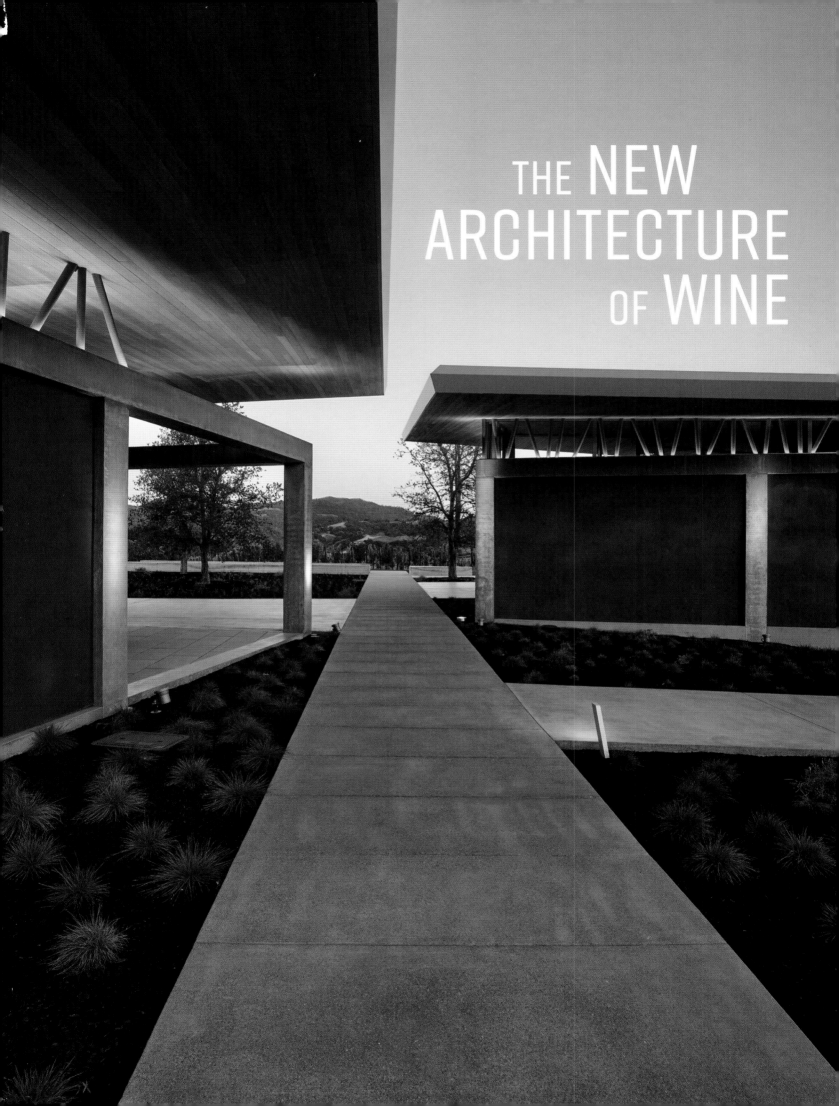

THE NEW ARCHITECTURE OF WINE

THE NEW ARCHITECTURE OF WINE

25 SPECTACULAR CALIFORNIA WINERIES

HEATHER SANDY HEBERT

GIBBS SMITH
TO ENRICH AND INSPIRE HUMANKIND

First Edition
23 22 21 20 19   5 4 3 2 1

Text © 2019 Heather Sandy Hebert
Illustrations © 2019 Donald Sandy
Photographic credits on pages 284–287
Front cover photograph © 2019 Matthew Millman
Back cover photograph © 2019 Casey Dunn

Published by
Gibbs Smith
P.O. Box 667
Layton, Utah 84041

1.800.835.4993 orders
www.gibbs-smith.com

Designed by Rita Sowins / Sowins Design
Printed and bound in China

Gibbs Smith books are printed on either recycled, 100%
post-consumer waste, FSC-certified papers or on paper
produced from sustainable PEFC-certified forest/con-
trolled wood source. Learn more at www.pefc.org.

Library of Congress Cataloging-in-Publication Data

Names: Hebert, Heather Sandy, 1961- author.
Title: The new architecture of wine : 25 spectacular
California wineries /
    Heather Sandy Hebert.
Description: First edition. | Layton, Utah : Gibbs Smith,
[2019]
Identifiers: LCCN 2018060091 | ISBN 9781423651390
(jacketless hardcover)
Subjects: LCSH: Wineries--California--History--21st
century. |
Architecture,
    Modern--21st century. | Architecture--California--
History--20th century.
Classification: LCC NA6422 .H43 2019 | DDC
720.9794/0904--dc23
LC record available at https://lccn.loc.gov/2018060091

FOR MY DAD, WHO INSPIRED MY LIFE-LONG PASSION FOR
ARCHITECTURE AND DESIGN.

FOR MY MOM, WHOSE DEVOTION AND UNWAVERING
SUPPORT HAS SPANNED A LIFETIME.

FOR MY CHILDREN, WHO ARE MY GREATEST JOY.

FOR MY HUSBAND, WHOSE BELIEF IN ME KNOWS NO BOUNDS
AND WHO GAVE ME THE CONFIDENCE TO FIND MY OWN VOICE—
YOU ARE MY EVERYTHING.

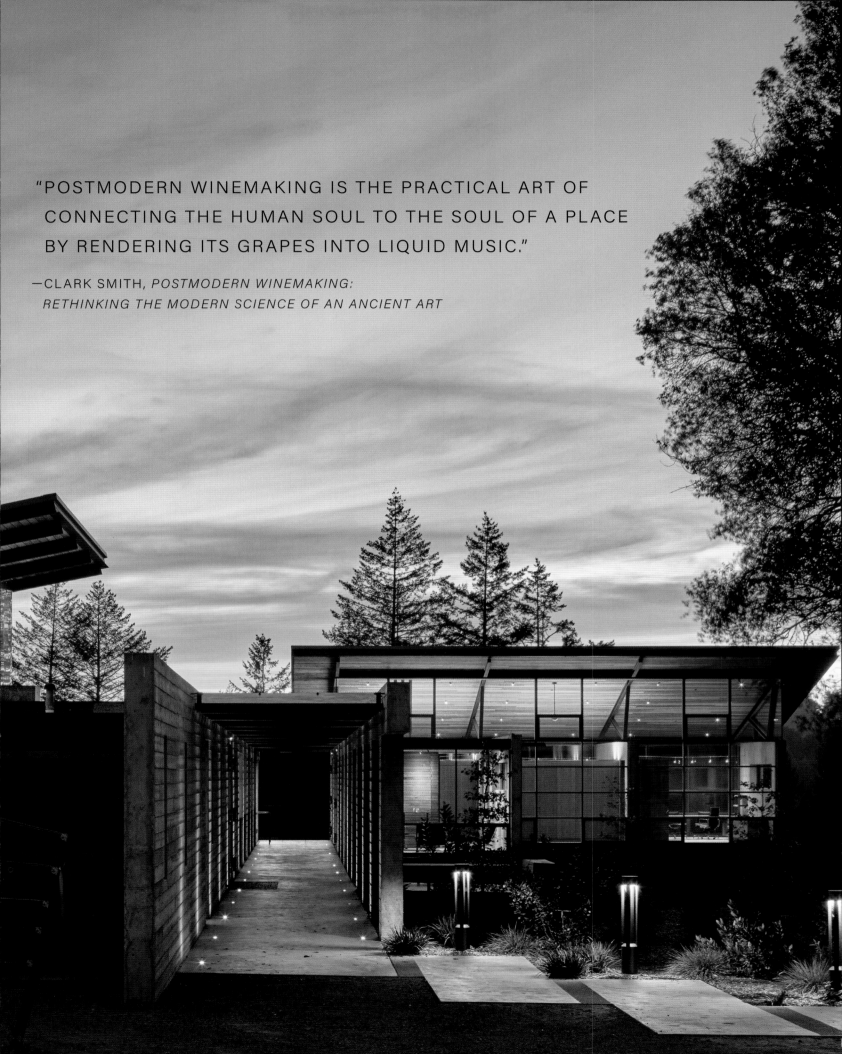

"POSTMODERN WINEMAKING IS THE PRACTICAL ART OF
CONNECTING THE HUMAN SOUL TO THE SOUL OF A PLACE
BY RENDERING ITS GRAPES INTO LIQUID MUSIC."

—CLARK SMITH, *POSTMODERN WINEMAKING:*
RETHINKING THE MODERN SCIENCE OF AN ANCIENT ART

CONTENTS

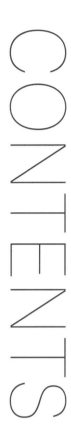

SUSTAINABILITY + LOVE OF THE LAND

SINGULAR VOICES

HISTORY REENVISIONED

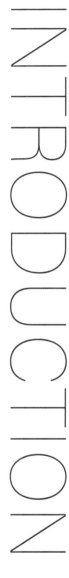

INTRODUCTION

We live in what Esther Mobley, wine editor for the *San Francisco Chronicle,* has called the "Golden Age of Wine." Long gone are the days when new-world wine had to prove itself against the pillar of old-world wine. The 40th anniversary of the famous Judgement of Paris, in which California wine asserted itself on the world stage, has come and gone. A new, second generation of vintners experiment and expand the definition of winemaking and the wine-making experience in California. And the lifestyle of California's wine country speaks to visitors from all over the world—old generation and new—in a common language based on immersive experience of the land and seasons, a commitment to sustainability, artisanship, and community and a sense of ease that comes from living your values.

Those values speak loud and clear in the new architecture of wine. In the last decade, winery architecture has come into its own in California. In place of the imitations of old-world estates or expressions of grandeur made for the sake of grandeur alone, California vintners and their architects are creating wineries as expressions of the place that California's wine country has become now, in its own right. Whether a modern expression of California's agricultural vernacular, a cutting-edge structure rendered in glass and steel, or a piece of wine country history reimagined in a contemporary style, the new architecture of wine expresses what the California wine country experience is right now.

No other type of commercial architecture embodies and expresses the passion of its inhabitants, their communion with the land, and their personal stories quite like winery design. Perhaps that is why most winery architects also specialize in residential design. These designers are adept at capturing their clients' aspirations, passions, and personal stories and expressing them through the medium of the built environment. This book is about the relationships between winemakers and the architects they trust to tell their story.

Howard Backen has distilled the essence of the agrarian winery building as it fits within the California landscape, so it is fitting that the first two wineries

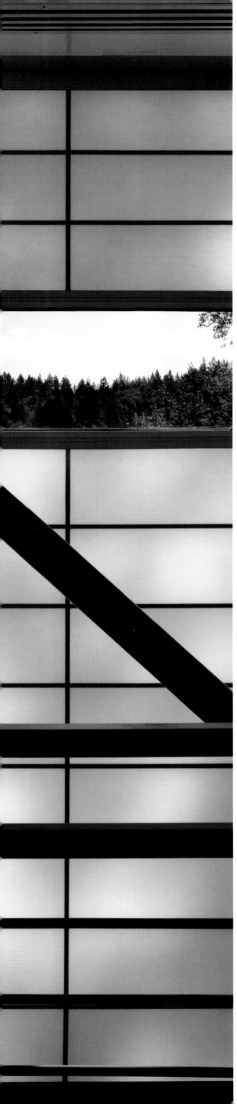

we visit in this book are designed by his firm, Backen & Gillam Architects. A charming man with an easy laugh that erupts frequently, Howard is still going strong at 82. Besides his architecture, perhaps his most lasting achievement is his role in defining the relationship between architect and client as far more than business. His clients become his lifelong friends. And a younger generation of architects is continuing that narrative. In story after story throughout this book, the relationships between architects and winemakers are those of trust, admiration, and shared enthusiasm for land, place, process, and artistry. Their work together is a mutual endeavor to live consciously and express what the land wants to say.

Winemaking is a ritual, an event at once agricultural, industrial, and artistic. Wineries are not just places to process grapes into wine. Nor are they places simply to visit to drink and buy wine. They are an opportunity for guests to immerse themselves in the world of winemaking, for a little while at least, and become a part of its community. This is what makes the architecture of wine so compelling. For everything here has a story behind it, which is part of the shared narrative of the California wine country.

Cycles of time within wineries are an important part of the ethos. Vineyards are developed, harvests come and go, each year providing the winemakers with a better understanding of their potential. Buildings must be built to last; then when and if needs change, they must be adapted to reflect the developing nature of the wine industry, winemaking process, and the visitor experience.

After spending a year taking a journey through some of the best new winery design in California, I have learned that every winery has a story and that no two stories are alike. More than any profession I have ever come across, the industry is about people: family and community knitted together in a passionate effort to create artistry through the land. So, while this book is a celebration of architecture and wine, it is also mostly about people.

I hope you enjoy the journey as much as I have.

THE NEW
AGRARIAN

RAM'S GATE WINERY

THE GATEWAY TO THE WINE COUNTRY

LOCATION: **CARNEROS**   ARCHITECTURE: **BACKEN & GILLAM ARCHITECTS**

Located amid the low-lying hills of the Mayacamas Mountain Range as they descend into the northern end of the San Francisco Bay, the 90 square miles of the Carneros wine region fall within both Sonoma and Napa counties. Cool and windy, this is the land of Pinot Noir, Chardonnay, and sparkling wines. Carneros—which in Spanish means "rams"—is truly the gateway to the wine country.

Set on the top of a prominent knoll at the southeast end of the Carneros region, on the primary route from the San Francisco Bay Area to the wine country, Ram's Gate is the first winery visitors encounter, visible on the hilltop for a good two miles before its gates come into view. Opened in 2011, Ram's Gate is the vision of four friends with a shared passion for wine, food, and hospitality: Michael John, Jeff O'Neill, Paul Violich, and Peter Mullin. But, insists managing partner Michael John, "Howard Backen is its soul."

When Michael John discovered the site for Ram's Gate, he was knee-deep in a career in private equity. But he had always thought that if the right property came on the market, he would like to invest in a winery—"a gorgeous place with world-class wines, where we could entertain friends and family and create a sense of community around

wine and food." The hilltop site, former home of Roche Winery, checked every box: the potential to plant 28 acres, majestic location, visibility, and proximity to San Francisco. Armed with a vision but lacking wine industry experience, Michael turned to Jeff O'Neill, an old friend and third-generation vintner who had spent his entire career in the wine industry as the former chairman of the Wine Institute and owner of O'Neill Vintners. They were soon joined by Paul Violich, an investor and agribusiness leader, and Peter Mullin, a businessman and passionate grape grower with vineyards in Italy.

The four partners, longtime fans of Howard Backen, enlisted his firm, Backen & Gillam Architects, to work with them on the vision for the winery. "Howard's luxurious agrarian aesthetic fits seamlessly into the wine country and Carneros in particular. His sense of design is timeless and connected to the site in a way that was really important to us," says Michael.

Along with Howard, they engaged Luca Pignata, a principal at Backen & Gillam Architects, to help them define their concept for the winery. "Howard is a visionary," says Michael, "but what Luca brought to the project was crucial for its success. With his Italian background and his understanding of the history of winemaking in Europe, he really helped us figure out what Ram's Gate should be. Howard's vision and Luca's background and attention to detail came together brilliantly."

The site for Ram's Gate seemed perfect, yet it had its challenges. The southernmost vineyard in the Carneros AVA, it would become a defining presence for the wine country. However, it also sits within sight and earshot of Sonoma Raceway, a major race track. And while the views of the Carneros hills, wetlands, and the San Francisco Bay are breathtaking, the winds are a factor to be reckoned with. Because of its prominent location, the winery draws a broad spectrum of visitors. "It's the most public winery we've ever designed," says Howard.

The group knew they wanted their visitors to feel that they had entered a different world and they would need to play an active role in defining it. They approached the project with open minds and a collaborative approach that allowed the design to evolve as they considered the site's opportunities and challenges. The result of that collaboration feels like a small village, a collection of indoor-outdoor structures circling a central courtyard. "This approach to winery design actually goes back centuries," says Luca. "The central core courtyard was where the grapes were collected and the wine was made, and it was also where the harvest was celebrated. This is a modern interpretation of that tradition—an age-old approach to hospitality."

Breaking the winery into numerous smaller structures also decreases the scale of the 22,000-square-foot winery so that it doesn't dominate its hilltop site. Composed of redwood board and batten stained to create a patina of age, the barn-like structures complete the trajectory of the hill's upward slope, an ode to the weathered farmsteads of old Carneros. The central courtyard forms the main entry to Ram's Gate. Anchored by a massive indoor-outdoor fireplace, the courtyard is the heartbeat of the winery. "The hearth as the hub of a house is almost universal," says Howard. To the left and right, soaring barns house the production winery and the primary tasting lounge. A gallery and glassed-in veranda connect the hospitality and production buildings, acting as a bridge between the making and celebrating of wine.

The culinary program was integral to the design brief from the outset. In order to create the world the partners envisioned, they needed to pair the wine with food. The main tasting room—with its soaring 30-foot ceilings, colossal cylindrical light fixtures, exposed rafters, and wood-clad walls—acts as a giant kitchen and living room. Dominated by an expansive bar of white marble and steel, it is fully open to the courtyard on one side and a south-facing terrace on the other.

The team's desire to create an abundance of indoor-outdoor spaces was balanced by a corresponding need to protect them from the elements, encapsulating them from ambient noise from the nearby raceway, and from the late-afternoon winds that are a part of life so close to the San Francisco Bay. Michael and Jeff challenged the team to come up with out-of-the-box thinking as they faced these challenges. Howard and Luca responded, and now the central courtyard is a world of its own, shaded by pistachio trees and shielded on all sides from the wind.

PREVIOUS OVERLEAF: Ram's Gate is designed around its central courtyard, which is the heartbeat of the winery and the first space visitors enter upon arrival.

ABOVE: The popular main tasting room is dominated by a marble tasting bar and opens completely to the courtyard.

OPPOSITE: The members library opens onto the barrel storage, providing a direct connection between the making and enjoyment of wine.

ABOVE: The courtyard acts as a central hub connecting the main tasting lounge, gallery, private tasting area, and barrel room.

ABOVE: Myriad spaces accommodate groups of six up to several hundred. Here, a cozy outdoor fireplace outside the members library seats six.

OPPOSITE: The member's library illustrates the winery's eclectic mix of sophistication and rusticity.

Glass doors on either side of the central hearth slide back, opening it up to the courtyard, while on the gallery's outer wall, a full wall of fixed glass welcomes in the vineyard views. Massive barn doors slide open or closed to reveal the production barn or to close it off. In a solution that has become emblematic of the winery's architectural style, huge steel-and-glass tilt garage doors lift up to transform the main tasting room into an uninterrupted indoor-outdoor space. Luca describes the balance required to make the doors work effortlessly as "a bit of a miracle."

Throughout the winery, spaces can be configured in numerous ways to accommodate groups ranging from six to several hundred, and there are multiple terraces on nearly every side. Along with the sweeping bar, the main tasting room includes a fireside tasting lounge and semiprivate chef's table. A members library adjacent to the production barn opens onto its own terrace and outdoor fireplace. A pond down the hill can be set up for tastings or picnics. "You can stay here the whole day," says Luca. "It is, to me, the most successful element of the design. You can see people staying for hours, making new friends."

The materiality of Ram's Gate creates a lasting impression. Weathered board-and-batten exteriors allow the buildings to blend into the landscape rather than calling undue attention to themselves. Interior walls clad in Douglas fir reclaimed from snow fences in Wyoming emphasize the winery's connection to the land by bringing exterior elements indoors. Reclaimed French granite pavers in the courtyard impart a sense of history. The mixture of rusticity and luxury is palpable, but equally important, it seems a concrete expression of the ownership group's dedication to creating an authentic experience and sense of place.

"That's the thing about winemakers," says Howard. "They are deeply connected to the ecology of the area, the land, and the place."

The gallery and glassed-in veranda act as a bridge connecting the making and the celebrating of wine. Outdoor terraces surround the collection of buildings.

Huge steel-and-glass tilt garage doors on either side of the primary tasting lounge open up to the central courtyard on one side and this expansive tasting terrace on the other.

DAVIS ESTATES

A FAMILY ROOM WITH A VIEW

LOCATION: **CALISTOGA**   ARCHITECTURE: **BACKEN & GILLAM ARCHITECTS**

Mike Davis has loved the Napa Valley for a lifetime. When he and his wife, Sandy, established their winery after a career in technology, they wanted nothing more than to invite people in to share in their enthusiasm for wine and food and the community that forms when you bring the two together. Visitors to the winery are tantamount to guests in their home. "We wanted it to be inviting, more like a family room than a living room," says Mike.

Mike grew up south of San Francisco, but his connection to the valley began early. Throughout his childhood, his family vacationed here in the summer, and Mike spent weeks camping, hunting, fishing, hiking, and cooking outdoors. His affection for the valley remained strong throughout his life. When it was time to sell their company, the couple's decision to move to the wine country and begin a second career in wine was a natural one.

In their search for the perfect site, Mike and Sandy looked at forty to fifty properties throughout the wine country. When they found a site just off the Silverado Trail in the northernmost region of the Napa Valley, they knew they had found it. The 155-acre site climbs from valley floor to 1,100 feet—a hillside site composed of eleven-million-year-old volcanic soil, historic structures, and one of the most spec-

tacular views in the valley. They loved the property's old barn, dating from 1916. They climbed the hill and sat in the vineyards. The property had everything: history, views, and good soil. "The combination knocked our socks off," says Mike.

Choosing an architect was far easier; every winery the couple admired was by Backen & Gillam. They asked Howard Backen and John Taft, a principal at the firm, to take the essence of the one-hundred-year-old barn and carry it through the new construction. The result is a collection of structures that is timeless—rustic and refined, old and new.

The assemblage of buildings is symmetrical, one side an exact mirror of the other. Set parallel to the adjacent Silverado Trail and slightly uphill from other buildings, the hospitality building presides over the site and might have threatened to overwhelm it had the team not thought to set the building deep into the hillside, reducing its scale. On either side of the symmetrical main building, the historic 1916 barn and the new production winery are set directly on axis, facing each other across the expansive courtyard. Clad in traditional board and batten siding stained a deep brown, the arrangement is collected and timeless, a true expression of the valley's agrarian tradition.

The main entrance is tactically placed at the rear of the building. The entry vestibule is lofty but restrained, separated from the soaring volume of the building's interior by massive steel doors that give no hint of the view awaiting on the other side. "I love a big reveal," says Mike, as he swings the doors open. The westerly view across the valley floor, to use Mike's words, "knocks your socks off."

The double-height central gathering space is flanked by an open kitchen and a cozy fireside tasting area reminiscent of a traditional inglenook, arranged in perfect symmetry. Though commercial in scale, the kitchen feels mysteriously like a very grand home kitchen. Tucked behind the kitchen, a private VIP tasting area has its own views, entry, and terrace. On the opposite end of the building, behind the fireside tasting area, administrative offices occupy a space laid out identically.

PREVIOUS OVERLEAF: Capacious hanging swings bookend the seating on the terrace at Davis Estate, providing the perfect vantage point to relax and take in the view.

ABOVE: The symmetrical hospitality building presides over the site, taking the essence of the property's historic barn and translating it into a contemporary wine-tasting experience.

The defining feature of the experience at Davis Estates is the view. Windows line the entire western facade, rendering that "knock your socks off" view visible from every inch of the interior. Glass doors across the central space peel back to connect to the terrace running the length of the room's western wall. Two sets of capacious swings, suspended from the rafters by steel rods, face each other across tables carved from blocks of cypress.

The hospitality building is a celebration of wood: cypress, cedar, pine, and walnut. Mike's grandfather was a furniture maker, and Mike inherited his passion for furniture design. He custom designed nearly every piece of furniture and had a hand in every detail. Steel beams clad in pine, walls and ceiling of rough-sawn cedar, and hand-hewn walnut floors warm the space. A single fallen monkeypod tree from Hawaii has been given new life as the central dining table, matching consoles on the terrace, and the huge circular table set within the expansive wine cave. In an ode to California's signature tree, a custom-designed rug interprets the play of light and shadow through the old oak trees that line the estate driveway.

Mike's influence is everywhere, from the custom-designed furnishings to the oversized chairs that had to pass his "sit test" to the windmill that graces the label, which he worked with Howard Backen to design. His multiple passions are on display in the historic barn, including antique tractors, a 1909 player piano, and a 1945 jukebox. Structurally reinforced and moved to align with the new winery production building, the barn now functions as an immensely entertaining event space.

Nowhere is Mike's passion for wine and entertaining on display more fully than in the wine cave. Tucked into the hill below the main building, a journey through the wine cave leads past wine fermenting in rows of oak and stainless steel, through a gallery lined with barrels and sculptures, to a set of solid steel doors. These doors are his biggest reveal: behind the doors, opened by a biometric vein hand scanner, an octagon of glass and steel sits within a library-in-the-round. The self-contained room is temperature controlled so that his guests can be comfortable within the cave, which is cooled to properly store the wines. Behind the enclosure, a discrete archway surrounds a piece of raw earth: the mountain's eleven-million-year-old volcanic ash, the ultimate juxtaposition of old and new.

As the cofounder of Applied Computer Solutions, Mike spent his career in technology, and he brings his lifetime of experience to bear here, using his fascination with technology to enhance his passion for winemaking. The winery incorporates an unprecedented level of technology. Everything is monitored and visible via a central program. In fact, Mike's team helped write the software with RTI (Refrigeration Technologies Inc.). Every system can be regulated via iPhone, from monitoring the oxygen levels in the tanks to controlling the property's fourteen separate music zones.

If there is a definitive example of client and architect having a roaring good time bringing a project to life, Davis Estates is that project. "This really was Mike's aesthetic," says Howard. "The scale echoes his personality. It's big and inviting, just like he is."

The cozy fireplace gathering space, with its deep leather-clad sofas, is reminiscent of a traditional inglenook.

Glass doors disappear out of sight, opening the entire western-facing facade to the view and making it nearly impossible to discern the line between the interior and the expansive covered terrace.

A choreographed journey takes visitors through the barrel room, down a gallery lined with a collection of sculptures, and then to a massive steel door that opens to reveal the cave and library-in-the-round.

TRINCHERO NAPA VALLEY

A TRIBUTE TO FAMILY

LOCATION: **ST. HELENA**   ARCHITECTURE: **BAR ARCHITECTS**

Trinchero Napa Valley commands a view of the Napa Valley shared by very few. Set upon a knoll at the narrowest point in this hourglass-shaped valley, it exists both within the valley and above it. Barely 30 miles in length, the Napa Valley is just 500 yards wide here. Surrounded by vineyards and cradled between Howell Mountain to the east and the forested slopes of Spring Mountain to the west, Trinchero Napa Valley gazes up valley directly toward Mount St. Helena.

The Trinchero family is one of the oldest and most successful wine families in the Napa Valley. Theirs is the second-largest family-owned winery in the United States, yet we don't recognize the name as we do the names Gallo or Mondavi—both scions of the industry—partially because the Trinchero family never put their name on their wine.

However, their brand—Sutter Home—is recognizable to all. In 1948, brothers John and Mario Trinchero, Italian immigrants, moved from New York to California in search of a better life. They purchased Sutter Home, which had been abandoned during prohibition. As hardworking farmers, their runaway success began in 1975 when, by a happy accident of stuck fermentation, they ended up creating white Zinfandel, which quickly became the most popular wine in the United States. The family wine business continued to grow, expanding to include other brands, and is now headed by Mario's sons Bob and Roger Trinchero. Following a dream to someday establish a winery honoring the family's wine-making history, the brothers started purchasing exceptional vineyards in the 1980s, and by 2007, they had acquired more than 200 acres of prime vineyards throughout the Napa Valley.

Then in 2004, the family purchased Folie a Deux, a charming winery midway between the wine-country towns of St. Helena and Calistoga. The purchase gave them the perfect home for Trinchero Napa Valley, which would be the family's first wine produced under the Trinchero family name. For the Trincheros, this wine and property are a celebration of the Trinchero history and a symbol of their vision for the future.

Bob Torres, principal, vice chairman, and director of Trinchero Family Wines—and a direct descendant of the founders—spearheaded the birth of Trinchero Napa Valley. Trained in architecture, he was deeply immersed in the development of the winery from start to finish, relishing the weekly meetings with his design team and playing an active role in design decisions large and small.

"My favorite part of the whole thing was being a part of the team and watching this thing come out of the ground," said Bob.

Built in three phases—the production winery came first, then the hospitality center, and finally the farmhouse tasting room—Trinchero Napa Valley feels like a small village of classic farmhouse structures surrounding a central gathering space. The plantings, which lean toward natives and mediterranean, fill every open space, while decomposed granite paths feel organic underfoot. This property is built for entertaining and the level of hospitality is extraordinary. Yet visiting feels as if Bob has invited you into his (very nice) home.

To bring his vision to life, Bob worked with San Francisco–based BAR Architects and Erin Martin Design, a design icon in the Napa Valley known for pushing the envelope on the wine hospitality experience. The resulting design juxtaposes simple, agrarian forms on the exterior with a sense of adventure and discovery within. The scale is bold, but not brash, and real warmth abounds.

Every space is layered and replete with history and significance. Everything has meaning, from the ship chains piled at the front door of the hospitality center as a tribute to Mario and John's arrival at Ellis Island to the taxidermy birds that alight in the tasting room to symbolize the dawn of a new generation. Bob and his wife Maria (a project manager for Erin Martin Design) worked closely with Erin, and every detail tells a story.

The hospitality center, which is open to the trade and employs a full-time culinary staff, pays homage to the family's roots. Bob points out numerous photographs of his grandparents who began the family's wine adventure. Not all the walls are what they seem to be; one wall in the tasting room is actually a concealed door leading to a hidden bar, decorated with cocktail recipes and filled with the family's estate spirits.

The demonstration kitchen feels like the most beautiful residential kitchen you've ever seen, at twice the scale. Off the kitchen, a casual indoor-outdoor seating area provides a private space for smaller food and wine pairings. Inscribed on the walls is the family's recipe for Bagna Cauda, a decadent Italian dish that Mario and Mary made to celebrate the end of harvest with family and employees, a tradition the family carries on to this day. Just beyond the steel bifold doors, a furnished terrace overlooks magnificent vineyard views and another outdoor entertaining space, furnished with picnic tables and a bocce ball court.

Erin Martin is known for her flair for the dramatic. Nowhere is it more evident than the lower-level candle room and wine cellar, which feels as if it lies in the bowels of a ship. Massive ropes and chains drape the walls. A wall of candles is

PREVIOUS OVERLEAF: At Trinchero Napa Valley, the interiors are layered with history and meaning, and it takes a while to soak it all in.

ABOVE: The straightforward farmhouse vernacular on the exterior belies the richly layered story told through the interiors.

ABOVE: Interior designer Erin Martin, well known for her flair for the dramatic, draped the lower-level dining room and wine cellar with ropes, chains, and a wall of candles.

OPPOSITE: The hospitality building feels like a private home, with an entry foyer leading to a living room lovingly furnished and filled with family mementos.

allowed to drip dramatically, and the wavering light from the oversized iron pendant lights and the multitude of candles creates an almost medieval atmosphere. All the details take a while to soak in. Only when you reach the end of the room and turn back do you notice the antique hat molds arranged in neat rows along the wall, or the arresting sight of an elephant's head in the stairwell.

The tasting room, which sits directly on the site of the former Folie a Deux tasting room, repeats the simple farmhouse vernacular—clean lines, horizontal siding, and a wraparound porch. But inside the doors a different world unfolds. Dark walls, wooden beams, curved leather banquets, and large-scale statues—every piece has a story—mingle with antiques selected to convey the Trinchero family narrative. Old football trophies and a collection of antique baseball bats reference the family's passion for sports. Antique books behind the tasting counter reference Mary's love of reading, and the perfect formula for wine is transcribed across the walls of the vestibule. A sly set of eyes painted on the door marks the entry to the Legacy Lounge, a VIP tasting room reminiscent of prohibition-era haunts. The highlight of the lounge is the speakeasy bar, a tribute to Mario, who worked as a bartender at New York's Barbizon Plaza and Waldorf Astoria just after Prohibition.

Appropriately, the winery's 22-acre site overlooks the Cabernet grapes of Mario's Vineyard. The family calls the wine made from those grapes "a tribute to the strength and perseverance of Mario Trinchero, who came to the Napa Valley with his family to realize the American dream."

BELOW: Lined with hand-tooled leather and filled with many of the family's estate spirits, the speakeasy bar was initially Erin Martin's idea, but it quickly became one of Bob Torres's favorite design elements.

OPPOSITE: The VIP Legacy Lounge lies behind the bar, accessed by a door painted with a sly set of eyes, in a playful nod to Prohibition-era speakeasies.

OPPOSITE: The 22,000-square-foot production winery was the first of the three structures to be built.

ABOVE: In the tasting room, everything tells a story: Books behind the bar reference Mary Trinchero's love of reading; a trophy case and antique baseball bats hint at the family's love of sports; and a taxidermy bird collection symbolizes new beginnings and the magic of the next generation.

MacROSTIE WINERY

A HOUSE FOR STEVE

LOCATION: **HEALDSBURG**   ARCHITECTURE: **GOULD EVANS**

After college, Steve MacRostie was headed for medical school when a stint in the army took him to Italy and changed his life. Traveling through Europe, he fell in love with the culture of food and wine. When his tour was over, he abandoned the safe route to medical school and decided to take the road less traveled, enrolling in the enology program at UC Davis. He had decided to become a winemaker.

However, becoming a winemaker was not the last time Steve would take the road less traveled. When he started making wine in 1974, as the inaugural winemaker for Sonoma County's Hacienda Winery, most young winemakers were headed to Napa to make the valley's famous Cabernet. Steve and a handful of others took a different path, heading to the fog-cooled vineyards of Sonoma County and their largely untapped potential to produce cool-climate varietals—Chardonnay and Pinot Noir.

In 1987, Steve went out on his own. Working with an array of grape growers to produce blends that reflect the entire Sonoma Coast, he has developed decades-long relationships and a devoted following for the pure and elegant style of his wines. With his relaxed charm and encyclopedic knowledge of Sonoma County, Steve is a natural host. He spent

the next twenty-eight years making wine in an industrial building in Sonoma, offering tastings in the chilly production facility. In 2015, Steve was finally able to give MacRostie Winery a home.

"I've always wanted a home for MacRostie that expresses who we are as a winery and what we believe in as clearly as our wines do," says Steve.

When Steve first met with his architect, Douglas Thornley of Gould Evans, he handed him a detailed design brief, all ready to go. He knew what he wanted. The final design—a play on residential forms—is entirely intentional. The design brief, jokes Douglas, was simple: "Make a house for Steve."

It is impossible to imagine a more perfect setting for a winery. The rolling hills gently converge to cradle the winery and estate house, surrounded on all sides by twenty-five acres of sustainably farmed vineyards. The hospitality and production buildings face each other across the central courtyard, shaded by the broad canopy of two existing sycamore trees. Steve wanted his guests to know that the property is also a working winery: the production building's glass doors open the barrel room to view. Clerestory windows and polycarbonate windows flood the working winery with light.

The Estate House feels more like a home than a business. The residential scale and furnishings reflect the winery's relaxed, personal brand of service, a direct extension of Steve and his wife Thale's personalities. Their goal is to create a genuine connection: each visitor is greeted in person with a glass of wine and treated as an invited guest. Lisamarie Kennedy, MacRostie's ebullient hospitality manager, hand selects hosts for each group based upon who the team feels would connect best with the group. The ebb and flow of winery personnel, and the many conversations going on, keep the atmosphere joyous and authentic. The winery's three dogs have the run of the place. This is a place where guests are meant to relax, kick back, and enjoy themselves.

The Estate House's modest scale and simple gabled form take their cues from Sonoma's traditional agrarian structures. Steve wanted a winery that was transparent and welcoming. Accordingly, Douglas's design clearly expresses its structural purpose, with nothing to disrupt the rhythm and flow of the architectural elements. A simple, refined palette of western red cedar, glass, blackened steel, and concrete reflects the materials traditionally used in winemaking. It is no accident that nearly everyone who opens the front door (strikingly composed of wood and set within the glass-front facade) stops short to take in the view straight through to the vineyards. "It never fails," laughs Lisamarie.

Interior designer Grant Gibson enhanced the residential character of the space with furnishings that soften the architecture and provide plenty of options for groups to linger: built-in sofas, a communal table, Danish camp chairs that are surprisingly comfortable, and abundant outdoor seating. The winery team affectionately refers to one particularly inviting outdoor sofa as the "five-hour couch" because guests have been known to linger there for hours. One of the most sought-after destinations is the "infinity table," set at the edge of the west terrace with nothing surrounding it but the view. Nine proposals have been staged at this table, and all were accepted, giving the winery a perfect record.

The atmosphere at MacRostie is communal; yet each setting within the winery offers a unique experience, no small feat given that, at 2,700 square feet, this is not a massive space. Every opening frames the views, and every vantage point seems better than the last. Terraces on three sides of the building effortlessly expand the lofty great room. The east terrace hovers above the valley floor, the south terrace showcases the adjacent rolling hills, while the north terrace features a combination of the two. The overhangs shading the north and south terraces are peeled back to reveal their underlying rafters, subtly transforming from roof to trellis, and prompting Steve to tease Doug, "So when are we going to finish the roof?" It's a story that both client and designer take great delight in telling.

MacRostie Winery opened in 2015 with six staff members, a number that had quickly expanded to twenty-eight by 2018. In the same short time period, the winery's club membership has grown from 128 members to 4,200, a testament to both their wines and the winery's genuine, heartfelt hospitality.

PREVIOUS OVERLEAF: The welcoming entry, where each guest is personally greeted with a glass of wine, provides a through view to the vineyards.

ABOVE: The west terrace is a popular spot and includes the famous "infinity table" and "five-hour couch."

"Architecture is not architecture until people inhabit it."
—Douglas Thornley

OPPOSITE ABOVE: Inspired by the massive doors typically used in airplane hangars, Douglas hung bifold doors horizontally so they open upward, creating a natural shade structure to shield the barrels within the production winery from the sun.

OPPOSITE BELOW: The transparency of the architecture translates to a lightness of being that shows through in photographs but is even more impactful in person.

ABOVE: A simple, refined palette of western red cedar, glass, blackened steel, and concrete reflects the materials traditionally used in winemaking.

MELKA ESTATES

ELEGANT DESIGN IN AN UNDERSTATED PACKAGE

LOCATION: **ST. HELENA**

ARCHITECTURE: **SIGNUM ARCHITECTURE**

Sometimes the most elegant design solutions come in small, understated packages. Such is the case at Melka Estates, just off Napa Valley's Silverado Trail. A simple form derived from the agricultural vernacular of the California wine country, the dark barn-like structure is nonetheless a dramatic fixture set against the green and gold hillsides of the Napa Valley. Humble and unassuming yet arrestingly beautiful, it is a perfect expression of the dynamism and the humility of both its owners and its architect.

Philippe and Cherie Melka and their architect, Juancarlos Fernandez, are perhaps three of the most recognized names in the Napa Valley, known for their talent, their intense commitment to their craft, and their humility. Maybe that is why they get along so well.

As business partners, the Melkas' pedigrees are lengthy. A native of Bordeaux, with a degree in geology and a master's degree in agronomy and enology from the University of Bordeaux, Philippe is as connected to wine and the land as it is possible to be. He began his career at the top, at Chateau Haut Brion, then worked with Moueix Company, Chateau Petrus, and numerous wineries in Italy and Australia. Armed with a degree in microbiology, Cherie began her wine-making

career at Ridge Vineyards, training under the legendary Paul Draper and working as the winery's enologist for five years. In 1991, their worlds came together with a chance meeting. While interning at Dominus, Philippe was visiting Ridge Vineyards to meet Paul Draper and taste his legendary wines when he walked into the lab and met Cherie. "Paul Draper was our matchmaker," laughs Cherie.

After spending a year and a half in France, the couple returned to the United States. Cherie worked with Beaulieu and Silver Oak Cellars. Philippe founded his company, Atelier Melka, and has spent over twenty years as a wine-making consultant to some of the Napa Valley's most prestigious family wineries, including Lail Vineyards, Dana Estates, Raymond, BRAND Napa Valley, and others. They cofounded Melka Estates in 1996, but it wasn't until 2017 that their wine venture had a home of its own.

The wine-making community in the Napa Valley is close and connected, as it is in the wine-making regions of Sonoma County and California's central coast. Since moving to the valley, the Melkas had lived in downtown St. Helena, raising two children and becoming deeply ingrained in the community.

PREVIOUS OVERLEAF: Melka Estates, with its simple yet arresting design, is a perfect expression of the dynamism and humility of both its owners and its architect.

ABOVE: A contemporary play on the traditional barn vernacular, the building is painted a deep shade of charcoal and grounded by the heritage oak that lies directly on axis with the structure's central breezeway.

But by 2011, they were looking for "less house, more land." A hillside site front-
ing the Silverado Trail, planted with two acres of Cabernet Sauvignon, offered just
what they were looking for. They began by building a house on the hillside—a
prefab modular home by Bay Area–based Blu Home—overlooking their vineyards
and the valley floor. Next, they worked with Juancarlos to renovate an existing barn
on the property to serve as a hospitality space with an airy upstairs tasting area,
and a large ground-level space for events. Juancarlos brought in Blasen Landscape
Architecture to tie the structures together with landscape.

"Juancarlos was our touchstone for everything here—the house, the renovated
barn, the new production winery, the landscape," says Cherie. "We don't make any
design decisions without him!"

They continued making their wine elsewhere until 2014, when they approached
Juancarlos about building a new production facility on the site. Completed in 2017,
the new winery is a simple barn-like structure with an emphasis on functionality
and efficiency. Set parallel to the adjacent Silverado Trail, it is comprised of two
prefabricated buildings painted a deep shade of charcoal. A landscaped berm lining
the front of the site runs visual interference between the winery and the adjacent
roadway. "The stealth dark color and the simplicity of the design reflects Philippe's
humble and reserved personality, but at the same time it makes a bold statement,
similar to the wines produced within the building," says Juancarlos.

The new winery totals just 2,000 square feet of interior space and 1,400 square
feet of covered exterior space. Three separate HVAC systems allow the wine-
making team to move the wine from place to place as it progresses through
fermentation and barrel aging—a French approach to the wine-making process.
Mobile cooling units can be relocated from place to place. "In a small winery, it's
all about efficiency," says Cherie.

Set on axis with the hospitality building, the two prefabricated structures that
comprise the production facility are augmented on nearly every side with covered
space formed by extrusions of the standing seam roof. Over the hospitality-facing
facade, a deep overhang creates a covered crush pad that Juancarlos calls "a modular cave." Two screened breezeways, one original and one added about a year later, provide flexible indoor-outdoor space along long facades to the east and west.
A motorized shade protects the western facade from the intense afternoon sun.

An existing oak tree to the east defines the winery's central point—the intersection of two strong axial relationships. Set on axis with the grand oak and
perpendicular to the road, a breezeway between the two structures forms a
vaulted cavern equally well suited for production or events. In fact, the flexible
spaces within the barrel rooms, under the extruded roofline and between the
hospitality and production buildings, provide a variety of areas for entertaining,
which the Melkas do often. "We have amazing events here," says Cherie.

The Melkas made their first vintage on-site in 2017, a fall season that saw some
of California's worst wildfires ever erupt in Napa and Sonoma counties. It was a
tough first harvest, but everything was saved. "We waited twenty years to do
this," says Cherie. "It was a long road getting here, but we're really happy."

The standing seam metal roof extends over the crush pad, forming a protected area for both winemaking and events.

ABOVE: The production winery's simple form is simultaneously comfortable within the landscape and dramatically set apart from it.

LEFT: Cherie found the light fixtures in the central breezeway at Erin Martin Design in downtown St. Helena and loves the way they turn in the breeze.

OPPOSITE: Under a concrete bench, a backlit screen echoes the portrait detail of Philippe that appears on the Melka Estates wine labels.

GRASSES + OAKS, GLASS + STEEL

QUINTESSA PAVILIONS

VALERIA'S VISION

LOCATION: **ST. HELENA** | ARCHITECTURE: **WALKER WARNER ARCHITECTS**

For Agustin Huneeus Sr. and his wife, Valeria, Quintessa is the culmination of a lifetime dedicated to wine. The property that would become Quintessa—a self-contained property that feels a world apart—was one of the last great unplanted properties in the Napa Valley, a land of forested hills and verdant valleys within the nearly flat expanse of land. Agustin Sr. puts it succinctly: "This special property seemed to be waiting for us to fulfill its destiny."

Before establishing Quintessa, Agustin devoted his entire professional life to winemaking, first in his native Chile, then as the head of worldwide operations for Seagrams, and later as the owner of numerous Napa Valley wineries. Valeria, a microbiologist and enologist who worked as a viticulturist in the Southern Hemisphere and later earned a degree in biochemistry, is an avid proponent of sustainable agriculture.

By all accounts, it was Valeria's perseverance and vision that enabled the couple to purchase the 280-acre property in 1989, when many before them had failed. The site is a tapestry of hills and swales, with a central lake that attracts a multitude of wildlife and birds. Valeria designed the vineyards and defined the approach to the land, planting forty small, sustainably farmed vineyard blocks in harmony with the varied topography.

The couple chose San Francisco–based Walker Warner Architects to plan the property and design the original winery. Though well known for its masterful residences, Walker Warner had never designed a winery, but their clients were unfazed. The firm had shown an affinity for the needs of the land and place that spoke to them. Carved into the hillside, and practically sited to save the best land for the vines, the original winery has garnered media attention and design awards for over a decade—its simple, organic beauty a hallmark of a new era of winery design in California. So, when the couple wanted to expand the visitor experience, they turned again to the team at Walker Warner, led by Greg Warner and Mike McCabe. Together they explored ways to expand the existing winery, but, in the end, prompted by the couple's wish to provide visitors with a deeper connection to the land, the architects took the experience outside.

It had long been the senior Agustin's custom to walk visitors through the vineyards, a journey that often took them up the hill above the winery via a pathway lined with oaks to the ridgeline, where

they could survey the undulations of the property. As Greg and Mike describe it, their job was to define the patriarch's walk with architecture.

Their solution took the form of three small, nearly transparent boxes—each only 250 square feet but surrounded by nearly 400 square feet of terrace—that nearly disappear into the landscape. Although they are nearly identical, each was specifically sited to maximize views and minimize disturbance of the native oaks. Slight variations in design and differing orientations make each pavilion experience unique.

Solid rear walls, rendered in highly textured board-formed concrete, block the pavilions from view until the very last moment. Entering through a small portal in the concrete wall, guests are immediately initiated into the full grandeur of the view, reinforcing the sense of discovery and connection with the land. Mike McCabe describes the experience as almost spiritual.

Slight in their dimensions, and restrained in palette, the pavilions belie the amount of thought that went into them. In a perfect marriage of simple lines, each element unfolds to either provide shelter from, or welcome in, the elements. Impossibly slim 2-inch-square columns hidden within the door frames are nearly invisible yet support the flat roofs that cantilever out over the terraces to provide shelter from the elements. The architects describe the pavilions as "Swiss Army knives of buildings," designed with precision to include everything they need and absolutely nothing they don't.

Though thoroughly contemporary, the pavilions incorporate subtle references to agrarian tradition, most notably in the massive slatted doors that slide open or closed across the 14 by 9-foot expanses of glass. The tonality and materials— glass and steel, roughly rendered board-formed concrete, and Napa Syre stone and natural wood—are driven by the terroir and impart a sense of refined rusticity. Materials and furnishings are spare and subtle. Sinker cypress derived from logs reclaimed from river bottoms lines the ceilings and defines the casework. Simple tables and accompanying benches are hewn from Afromosia, an African teak certified by the Forest Stewardship Council (FSC). Landscaping is limited to drought-resistant native grasses.

With the new pavilions, Walker Warner has created a deeper connection between the winery and the guest, providing a journey through the land that means so much to the couple, who have poured their heart and soul into the land. The design of the pavilions carries on the tradition of stewardship that began when Valeria first planted vines here. Although she is no longer in the fields every day, she remains Quintessa's vineyard master. This property is her vision.

PREVIOUS OVERLEAF: Carefully sited amid the oak trees, the three diminutive structures that comprise the Quintessa Pavilions are nearly invisible from the opposite hillside.

ABOVE: Though thoroughly contemporary, the pavilions incorporate subtle references to agrarian tradition, most notably in the massive slatted doors that slide open or closed across the 14- by 9-foot expanses of glass.

"Sinker cypress," derived from logs reclaimed from river bottoms, lines the ceilings and defines the casework; simple tables and accompanying benches are hewn from Afromosia, an African teak certified by the Forest Stewardship Council.

BELOW: The huge slatted screens, which can be slid open or closed, create a striated pattern on the pavilion wall.

OPPOSITE: There is a sense of luxury in the spareness of the architecture and in the way each pavilion feels completely private, as if it were sitting all alone on the ridge.

OCCIDENTAL WINES

ON THE EDGE OF THE CONTINENT

LOCATION: **OCCIDENTAL** | ARCHITECTURE: **NIELSEN:SCHUH ARCHITECTS**

Perched on the far western edge of the continent, five miles from the California coast, the ridge where Steve Kistler lives and works is a sort of Shangri-la—the culmination of a lifelong dream for one of California's most revered winemakers. A man of few words, Steve says simply, "I wouldn't trade this ridge for anyplace on earth."

Steve Kistler's grandfather, a collector of wines, exposed Steve to great wines of the world from a very young age. So it was not entirely out of the blue that, after graduating from Stanford with a degree in English, Steve took a job at Ridge Vineyards. Training under Paul Draper, one of the world's most celebrated winemakers, he proceeded to learn the business from the ground up and absorb the natural, minimalist approach to winemaking that would come to define his career. After just three years, Steve founded Kistler Vineyards in the heart of Sonoma County and quickly became a legendary name in the wine business in his own right. He remained at the helm of Kistler Vineyards until 2017, when he stepped down to follow his dream of producing coastal Pinot Noir with his two daughters, Catherine and Lizzie.

Steve's attraction to California's coastal ridges began early. When he started at Ridge Vineyards,

far inland in Santa Clara County, one of his duties was to drive toward the coast to pick up grapes from vineyards in Sebastopol, a mere eight miles inland from where Occidental Wines now stands. At the time, Sebastopol was the far western edge of grape-growing, and the quality of the land there fascinated him. "What attracts me most to these ridges is the way the wines speak of where they come from," says Steve. "You can sometimes even detect the salinity that comes in on the sea air." For years, he held this western edge in the back of his mind, knowing he would someday return.

In 2008, he began accumulating land, assembling parcels that would grow to some 250 acres, 85 of them farmed to produce Occidental's estate-grown Pinot Noirs. Three years later, he released his first bottling under the Occidental label. He built a house on the site, putting down roots both literally and figuratively. When it came time to build the winery, he knew he wanted to work with a local architect so he could play an active role in the design process.

Without hesitation, he turned to Amy Nielsen and Richard Schuh, of Sonoma-based Nielsen: Schuh Architects. Amy, Richard, and Steve connected immediately, and by all accounts, the

PREVIOUS OVERLEAF: A covered loggia links the hospitality building and the administrative offices.

ABOVE: Linked by the covered loggia, the hospitality and administration buildings are delicately rendered in glass and steel, with rooflines that seem to hover above the weighty concrete walls.

What might have been a stark space of glass and concrete is rendered warm and inviting by a long, low fireplace and the glow of reclaimed redwood.

collaboration was seamless. Unassuming and modest, Steve wanted a structure that was straightforward, agricultural, very transparent, and, above all, intimately connected with the land. "He came to us with the program meticulously thought out. He has been thinking about this, about creating a bespoke space for winemaking from the ground up, for his whole career," says Amy. Richard adds, "Steve is more personally committed to his craft than anyone I've ever met in the wine business. He just needed to work with us to build the architecture around that process."

Steve sat down with the team every week and was involved in every detail. The resulting structures, with their restrained palette and purity of architectural expression, are a direct reflection of his approach to winemaking. "It is so satisfying to me to have built something that has the simplicity and transparency that we strive for in our wines," says Steve.

The land here at the edge of the continent tends to rolling hills, covered in grasses and punctuated by oaks, manzanitas, and groves of evergreens. The coastal fog rolls in and retreats with a regularity that virtually assures cool mornings and warmer afternoons. The two separate structures housing the hospitality/administrative offices and winery production are carefully sited to fit into the hillside, their canted rooflines echoing the slope. Their primarily horizontal planes exist in marked contrast to the surrounding forest, which is dominated by the vertical spires of Douglas firs. Though different in scale and use, the architects achieved a distinct harmony between the two structures. Set higher on the slope, the hospitality building overlooks the vineyards on three sides, while the winery below is set deep into the hillside, seeming to grow out of the land itself.

The production building is set entirely below grade. The floor of the barrel room, which comprises roughly a third of the building's footprint, is constructed 35 feet below the natural slope. The placement of the barrel room below ground level was a driving decision for the winery, as it creates optimum conditions for cellaring of the wine. Above grade, the team reestablished the relationship with the hillside, canting the roofline at a pitch a bit steeper than the existing slope to let the light flood in through the clerestory windows. The standing seam metal roof is covered in a solar array, which generates most of the electricity to run the winery. The west-facing roofs make the most of the afternoon sun that, in this coastal area, is more predictable than the often fog-shrouded mornings.

Just up the hillside, two smaller structures house a tasting room and administrative offices. Linked by a covered loggia, these elegantly simple structures are a dance of opposites, the tension between the weighty concrete structures and the delicate roof structures entirely intentional. Held aloft by slender steel posts, the rooflines seem to hover above the walls, allowing clerestory windows to bathe the interiors with natural light. The loggia, composed of a repeating pattern of concrete portals, is a work of art in itself. Folded Corten steel plates let in light, but trap rain from above, producing a delicate play of light and shadow on the ground below.

Within its board-formed concrete frame, the tasting room is composed almost entirely of glass. The result is a tasting experience that is viscerally entwined with

The entry to the main tasting lounge frames the view of the vineyards just on the other side of the windows, highlighting the immersive nature of the experience.

the visual experience of the vineyards. What might have been a stark space of glass and concrete is rendered warm and inviting by a long, low fireplace and the glow of redwood, reclaimed from a decommissioned airplane hangar in nearby Sacramento. The palette of materials—comprised almost entirely of concrete, glass, steel, and reclaimed redwood—is perfectly attuned to the grasses, oaks, and manzanita that cover the hillsides. To keep the effect seamless, the architects custom designed many of the most important furniture pieces, such as the desks and the long tasting table.

Amy and Richard wanted their buildings to be an inspiration for their client. For Steve, the land speaks through the wine. For Amy Nielsen and Richard Schuh, the land speaks through the architecture. It is a perfect pairing.

OPPOSITE: The architects custom designed many of the furnishings and cabinetry to maintain an entirely seamless aesthetic.

ABOVE: A quiet patio emphasizes the connection between the restrained palette of materials and the grasses, oaks, and manzanita that cover the hillsides.

Set deep into the hillside, with a roofline canted just slightly more than the adjacent grade, the production winery benefits from thermal cooling and natural light that flows through the clerestory windows.

PROGENY WINERY

A SPIRITUAL CONNECTION TO THE LAND

LOCATION: **MT. VEEDER** ARCHITECTURE: **SIGNUM ARCHITECTURE**

Progeny Winery's new hospitality building is a small, light-filled jewel box set within the mountainous terrain of the Mt. Veeder AVA. Located on 260 acres high in the hills, up a driveway that measures exactly a mile, the land feels a world apart from the valley just below. "It's 7 minutes from Highway 29," says founder Paul Woolls, "and yet when you get here you feel like you're in another country."

Paul and Betty Woolls have owned this land—a former cattle ranch—since 2007. In fact, they went into contract the same weekend they were married. Betty already owned a successful winery on Howell Mountain but this piece of land, brought to their attention by a friend, was too beautiful to pass up. Mt. Veeder's steep slopes and minimal topsoil are rugged and challenging, but renowned for producing intense, age-worthy wines. When the couple purchased the land, they didn't know if it held enough water to grow grapes successfully, but they went ahead with the purchase anyway. "We decided if we found water, we'd plant a vineyard," Paul explains. "If not, we'd have a really wonderful place to walk around."

They found water. "And here we are," says Paul with a smile.

The couple planted their first vines in 2009, harvested their first crop in 2012, and introduced their first vintage in 2015. In 2016, they completed construction on their winery production facility. Elegant in its simplicity, the production facility sits unobtrusively against a stand of trees, a straightforward design solution comprised of two prefabricated structures sited and detailed by architect Juancarlos Fernandez of Signum Architecture. Just as the production winery was completed, construction crews broke ground on the new hospitality building.

For the hospitality building, the couple turned again to Juancarlos Fernandez. "They had a tremendous amount of faith in my instincts," says Juancarlos. "They admired contemporary architecture, and they knew they did not want a barn. Other than that, they were open to new ideas." There was a great deal of trust and alignment between client and architect. Paul recalls: "We gave him a bottle of wine, he came up to the site—I think he was on his bike—and he sat and looked for a long time."

Architect and client studied the land together to determine the best site for the new building. They considered building it near the massive oak tree that provides the inspiration for both the winery's name

PREVIOUS OVERLEAF: Progeny Winery is set upon a knoll overlooking rolling hills and vineyards high up in the Napa Valley's Mt. Veeder AVA.

ABOVE: Set askew from the skeleton and roof, the two structures feel like small glass jewel boxes dropped at an angle into their concrete frames, shielded from the sun by broad overhangs.

OPPOSITE: Slim structural posts, interspersed with posts of rusted steel salvaged from the ends of vineyard rows, allow the roofs to float above the walls.

ABOVE: The concept was to split the building into two structures, with rooflines just four feet apart, that seem to merge into a single building when viewed from a distance.

and its label, which features a sketch of the centuries-old tree. The sketch gives equal weight to the branches, which reach skyward, and the roots, which dig deep into the earth, emphasizing the concept of the land as progenitor. But even with its views of the Napa Valley to the east, the site was best suited for quiet inspiration, so they simply placed large picnic tables beneath the oak tree and left it otherwise untouched. They decided to set the new hospitality building on a knoll just up the hill from the production winery, overlooking the property's undulating vineyard-covered hills.

Juancarlos conceived the initial design and presented it to Paul and Betty. "I presented this crazy idea for the winery, and they loved it," Juancarlos recalls.

His concept was to split the building into two smaller structures. The two buildings—with roof lines separated by just four feet—loosely represent Paul and Betty. One houses the tasting areas and kitchen, while the other holds private offices. From a distance, the rooflines seem to join together, in perfect harmony with the adjacent hillsides, and with each other. The roof lines, which appear long and low when seen from afar, soar above the diminutive structures, held aloft by a concrete exoskeleton that brings to mind a modern-day stonehenge. The concrete skeleton and roof are set on axis with Mt. Veeder to the west; the structures within are oriented toward the vineyard view to the northwest. Set askew from the skeleton and roof, the structures feel like small, glass jewel boxes dropped at an angle into their protective concrete moment frames, shielded from the sun by broad overhangs.

Juancarlos wanted to create something new and something old at the same time. To that end, the raw concrete will age more quickly than the glass-walled structures, giving the concrete structure a sense of gravitas over time. The structural concrete frames were formed by custom-mixing the concrete into a nearly liquid form, an incredibly tricky process. Since the skeleton literally holds everything up, there could be no air pockets between the concrete and the steel set within it. "The margin for error was about zero," says Juancarlos. The construction team left no room for error, creating a mock-up before embarking on the actual frame. Leaving nothing to waste, the team placed the concrete mock-up within a grove of trees near the production winery, on axis with the vine rows. Two low concrete walls directly on axis with the arch forge a connection between the winery and hospitality buildings, and invite visitors to take a walk in the vineyards.

Slim structural posts, interspersed with posts of rusted steel salvaged from the ends of vineyard rows, allow the roofs to float above the walls. They also create a tactile connection between the building and the steel posts anchoring the vineyard rows just beyond the expansive terrace. Clad in white and light wood, and flooded with natural light, the interiors are cleanly furnished, giving Progeny the serene, zen-like quality of a gallery.

"I like the simplicity of modern design," says Paul, whose mid-century home in LA was designed by architect Richard Lim in the 1960s. "There is a oneness with the site that comes with very good architecture that is almost spiritual. I felt that spiritual connection in my LA home. I feel it here too."

Architect Juancarlos Fernandez envisioned the interior as a gallery space, a clean and elegant backdrop for the wine and views.

OPPOSITE: The furnishings, by Anthony Flesher Interiors, are clean, polished, and inviting.

ABOVE: Expansive glass doors fold back to connect the private dining area to the views of the infinity pool and vineyards.

Set just off the demonstration kitchen and private dining area, an infinity-edge pool reflects the adjacent vineyards and provides an artful transition between the contemporary design and the landscape.

PRESQU'ILE WINERY

A SENSE OF SOUTHERN HOSPITALITY

LOCATION: **SANTA MARIA**   ARCHITECTURE: **TAYLOR LOMBARDO ARCHITECTS**

In French Creole, *presqu'ile* means "almost an island"—the perfect name for a winery perched lightly on the ridgeline, very nearly an island amid the vineyards. With its clean, contemporary lines and butterfly roofline, Presqu'ile Winery seems about to take off in flight.

Set atop the Santa Maria Mesa in northern Santa Barbara County, Presqu'ile is quite unlike any other winery in this part of the state, set apart not only by its remarkable architecture but by its weather: cool, breezy, and often foggy. Located on 240 acres once deemed too cool to grow grapes, Presqu'ile is one of the westernmost wineries on California's central coast and benefits from the only two transverse mountain ranges—running east-west rather than north-south—on the western coast of the Americas. This rare convergence of geography and geology creates a natural funnel, drawing cool air off the Pacific Ocean, which, combined with one of the longest growing seasons in California, shapes a true cool-climate, wine-growing region.

The site is nothing short of spectacular. Panoramic views run all the way from the eastern to the western borders of the Santa Maria AVA, with vistas of Santa Maria Valley to one side and the Pacific Ocean on the other. "Once we opened, all

the Santa Maria locals said they had no idea these views existed," says president Matt Murphy.

Presqu'ile was built as a family business: a multigenerational collaboration between Madison and Suzanne Murphy, their children, Matt, Anna, and Jonathan, and their daughters-in-law, Amanda and Lindsey. Like so many residents of the California wine country, they hail from parts beyond, with deep roots in agriculture: four generations of Murphys farmed land in Louisiana. Matthew Murphy's great-grandfather established a beloved family compound on the Mississippi Gulf Coast, naming it Presqu'ile, after a point that projected almost like an island into the gulf.

When Presqu'ile was destroyed in 2005 by Hurricane Katrina, the family decided to restart out West, following oldest son Matt, who had already fallen in love with the wine business in California. Led by Matt, the family searched for the ideal site to establish a foothold and plant Pinot Noir. In 2007, they purchased their coveted estate, just sixteen miles from the Pacific Ocean. The estate is a tapestry of vineyard blocks, all sustainably certified. In honor of the compound they had lost, they named it Presqu'ile. This was their Presqu'ile West.

From the beginning of the family's collaboration

The architects designed the composed collection of structures, set on and just below the ridgeline, to create a journey through the winery with multiple points of discovery.

with San Francisco's Taylor Lombardo Architects, the synergy was obvious. The site had no infrastructure, so they built everything from the ground up. Tom Taylor and his partner, Maurice Lombardo, bushwhacked their way through the site to find the perfect placement for the buildings. Tom recalls, "The family gave us a great deal of leeway to express what the land wanted to say."

"It was a pretty monumental undertaking considering there was no preexisting infrastructure," says founder Madison Murphy. "The fact we are still friends after such an undertaking is a testament to the professionalism and good nature of the team."

The design process revolved around three principles. First, the architecture should reflect winemaker Dieter Cronje's clean, minimalist approach to wine. Second, as self-proclaimed evangelists for the Santa Maria Valley, the Murphys wanted to create an architectural landmark for the region. Finally, and most importantly, the winery should embody the family's sense of warmth and Southern hospitality.

Matt and Dieter met while working with other vintners, bonded over their love of Pinot Noir, and in 2008 came together to establish Presqu'ile. Both believe in maintaining the purity of the wine-making process, working sustainably with the land, and letting the grapes and terroir speak for themselves. Consequently, gravity is the organizing principle: the force of gravity moves both the grapes and wine through the winery, a process that is gentler on the grapes and stingier in its use of power. At Presqu'ile the grapes begin on the crush pad atop the ridge and eventually end up 110 feet below in the barrel cave.

This vertical orientation, combined with the dramatic ridgeline site, allowed the architects to craft a series of structures, weaving together hospitality and production and creating a journey through the winery. There is a "Wow" moment virtually every step of the way, but the crescendo comes with the ascent to the upper terrace, mounted atop the hospitality building directly level with the crush pad.

"Guests come through the gates and wind their way up to the property as the building comes into view. They enter at the lower level with a view straight into the cave, then travel up through the winery having no idea of the heroic view that awaits them when they reach the upper level. It's amazing," says Maurice.

The winery was designed to accommodate the full force of Southern hospitality. The plan is open and fluid; broad terraces accommodate large parties; indoor and outdoor fireplaces invoke warmth even on the chilliest days; and flexible furnishings can be rearranged for varying uses. An outdoor amphitheater overlooking the Pacific can hold up to 700 people, but the grassy venue is beautiful even when not in use. The winery hosts live music every Friday, and at least ten large music events a year.

Presqu'ile is built upon a foundation of family, friends, and authentic hospitality. "Winery design has evolved," says Maurice. "Hospitality has become the center of the experience."

OPPOSITE ABOVE: The view from the upper-level observation terrace is the winery's ultimate "wow" moment.

OPPOSITE BELOW: Carved into the landscape, the amphitheater looks out over the views toward the ocean and can seat up to 700 people.

ABOVE: Terraces surround the hospitality building.

In contrast to the view-oriented terraces at the front of the building, the rear terrace is intimate, with multiple spots to gather.

BELOW: The interiors are warm and inviting with flexible furnishings that can be rearranged to accommodate events.

OPPOSITE: Interior walls are lined in Lompoc stone, native to central and southern California, which is hand cut and laid by a single craftsman.

CUVAISON ESTATE

A STORY OF EVOLUTION

LOCATION: **CARNEROS**   ARCHITECTURE: **GOULD EVANS**

The story of Cuvaison is a story of evolution. Founded by a pair of scientists in 1969, Cuvaison originally made its home in Calistoga, in the upper reaches of the Napa Valley. In 1979, the winery's destiny shifted when it was purchased by the Schmidheiny family of Switzerland. The family, which made its fortune in concrete and building materials over several generations, also had a deep history in wine.

Thomas Schmidheiny, the grand-nephew of the family company's founder, owns wineries in Switzerland, Argentina, and California. His grandfather founded a wine growers cooperative and his father started making wine on the family's Heerbrugg estate when Schmidheiny was a child. In 1979, it was Mr. Schimdheiny's mother who, after a visit to California, suggested investing in winemaking here. This led to the purchase of Cuvaison, and to the purchase of 390 acres in the Carneros region—a decision that would profoundly shape the growth and direction of both Cuvaison and Carneros. At that time, the region was mostly dairy country. Yet, sensing the potential offered by the region's rolling hills and bay-cooled breezes, the family began planting in 1980, focusing on the cool-climate varietals for which the winery is now known.

For many years, Cuvaison maintained its footing in both Calistoga and Carneros, but it was increasingly clear that the winery belonged in Carneros. In the early 2000s, Cuvaison constructed a production facility on the Carneros land. The large structure, designed in a straightforward agricultural vernacular, allowed them to process their grapes, farmed in small-lot batches, under one roof. The next step was to bring hospitality and administration to Carneros. Douglas Thornley, of Gould Evans, helped Cuvaison create a pair of structures to complement the simplicity of the winery production facility, working closely with former Cuvaison president and CEO Jay Schuppert, who has since retired. Douglas and his team conceived a wine-making campus that places visitors squarely in the midst of the wine-making process, yet simultaneously allows them to feel visually and viscerally connected to the land.

"We wanted to continue to unlock what is in the land," says Dan Zepponi, the new president and CEO of Cuvaison Wines. "We have farmed the land in Carneros for decades, and we are now unlocking the human experience."

The winery campus is set at the top of a rise in the middle of the vast property. Cuvaison vineyards

lie in all directions. "This is the soul and heartbeat of the winery," says Dan. "There are hundreds of acres here, and we are right in the center of it."

The two newest buildings are very contemporary for a legacy brand; Cuvaison celebrates fifty years in 2019, a tangible symbol of the brand's rebirth in the Carneros region. Rendered in aluminum, glass, and cedar, the buildings are designed to create a dialogue with the functional design of the production buildings and take a back seat to the surrounding vineyards. The 9,350-square-foot rear building provides barrel storage, offices, and a wine library. The vaulted second floor blending room allows VIP guests and visiting distributors a view of the barrel room below and southwestern views of the vineyards.

The new hospitality building is the public face of Cuvaison, designed for a dedicated and growing group of wine club members. It faces northwest, overlooking Milliken Peak, the rolling hills, and an impossibly picturesque pond used to capture rainwater for reuse. With a distinct foreground, middle ground and background, it is a layered view, and the quality of the light is akin to a painting. In fact, when the three buildings come into view along the mile-long driveway, they assemble themselves in a similar fashion—a complementary composition of foreground, middle ground and background. Although the Sonoma Highway (which connects the Sonoma and Napa Valleys) is just a mile away, it cannot be seen or heard from the winery.

The 2,350-square-foot hospitality building announces itself with a covered breezeway that tilts jauntily skyward—a welcoming gesture that, when seen in concert with the aluminum stairway, creates a funnel of sorts that draws visitors toward the building. The structure is small in stature, sheathed inside and out with horizontal cedar siding, and in direct contrast to the silvery sheen of aluminum. A shed roof is angled to capture the views to the northwest and bring every bit of available light into the building.

The open-plan interior is primarily comprised of a single space, which can be closed off with partially frosted glass doors to create a separate, smaller space for VIP tastings and events. Walls of glass recede to render the delineation between indoors and outdoors virtually indiscernible. The cedar lining the ceiling and stone pavers on the floors flow unchanged from indoor spaces to the outer terrace, reinforcing the commingling of inside and outside experiences. Alongside the warmth of the wood and the cool hues of the slate floors and aluminum framing around the doors and windows, the green of the vineyards defines the color palette of the interiors. Coastal breezes, morning fog, and the varying color of the light all shape the landscape and are reflected in the interior, subtly transforming it in different seasons and at different times of the day. Regardless of the season or time of

PREVIOUS OVERLEAF: The pivoting front door at
Cuvaison welcomes in both visitors and the view.

ABOVE: The hospitality building announces itself with
a covered breezeway that tilts jauntily skyward.

LEFT: Design details like these wine shelves are rendered with a distinctly Danish sensibility.

OPPOSITE: The new hospitality building is small in stature and sheathed with horizontal cedar siding, in direct contrast to the silvery sheen of aluminum.

day, the primary impression is one of complete transparency. "When it's cool out, we can close all the windows, and our guests still feel like they are outside," says Daniel. "It is that transparent."

Douglas and his team, who were also responsible for the interiors, stuck to furnishings simply rendered in wood and aluminum, with plush sofas in tones of steel gray in the VIP lounge. Evidence of Douglas's training in Denmark, the clean-lined aesthetic is serene, and nothing competes with the view. Douglas chose the ceiling lights in the main tasting room—soft white orbs with a faintly midcentury quality—because they would move in the breeze, a reminder of the forces of nature at work just outside. The frosted glass doors that slide closed to delineate the VIP tasting area are only partially frosted, leaving bands of clear glass at the tops and bottoms of the doors, just enough to create a sense of curiosity while maintaining privacy for those within.

Terraces surround the building on two sides, dramatically expanding the sense of space. Glass sliding doors peel back to open up the entire corner of the tasting room to the broad terrace, creating a contiguous flow between indoors and out. Furnished with low-slung seating and bounded by low walls (which can function as additional seating when needed), the terraces provide a front-row seat for the vineyard views. "This is the kind of place where people want to hang out, where they feel they belong," says Douglas.

The Calistoga property is now sold, and Cuvaison has everyone under one roof—or more accurately, under three roofs—in Carneros. They have 3,500 people in the wine club and that number continues to grow. Accordingly, Daniel and Douglas have reconnected to talk about expanding the hospitality space, perhaps stepping the terraces further down toward the vineyards to create more outdoor experiences on the view, among other ideas. "We are fifty years old, but we're still evolving," says Dan. "We started in a cave in Calistoga, and now we're on the top of the hill in Carneros. We couldn't be happier."

OPPOSITE: The vibrant green of the surrounding vineyards becomes as much a part of the interior color scheme as the cedar lining the walls and ceiling, or the stone pavers on the floors.

ABOVE: Walls of glass lining two of the building's four walls recede to render the delineation between indoors and out virtually indiscernible.

SUSTAINABILITY + LOVE OF THE LAND

HALL WINES

A CELEBRATION OF WINE, ART AND PEOPLE

LOCATION: **ST. HELENA** ARCHITECTURE: **SIGNUM ARCHITECTURE**

When Kathryn and Craig Hall first sat down to discuss the design for their new winery with Jarrod Denton, cofounder of Signum Architecture, they asked him to create something different, something no one had ever seen in the Napa Valley. They also wanted to honor their site's roots in the valley's winemaking tradition, provide a museum-quality backdrop for their world-class collection of contemporary art, and build a winery that expressed their devotion to sustainability and love of the land. Above all, they wanted the winery to reflect their personality, and become a place to entertain on a grand scale.

"We love to entertain," says Kathryn Hall. "It's in our DNA."

The best architects love a challenge, and the Halls had certainly provided it. Jarrod responded with a winemaking campus that pairs a meticulous reimagining of a historic structure, with a seminal structure that is at once a production winery, art gallery, hospitality center, and setting for some of the valley's most notable events, such as Auction Napa Valley. He also succeeded in designing California's first LEED Gold-certified winery, finishing just ahead of his partner, Juancarlos Fernandez, whose LEED Gold-certified design for

CADE Winery was completed a week or so later.

Kathryn Hall grew up amid her family's vineyards in nearby Mendocino and had long dreamed of creating a destination in the Napa Valley to celebrate her love of wine, art, and entertaining. In 2003, she and Craig took the first step toward pursuing that dream by purchasing a plot of land with deep winemaking history: it housed the historic Peterson-Bergfeld Winery and a collection of other structures. Set in the heart of the Napa Valley just below the town of St. Helena, the prominent site offered them the opportunity to create an iconic destination amid the many wineries on the valley floor.

Originally constructed in 1885, the Peterson-Bergfeld building is one of California's best-known ghost wineries—pre-prohibition wineries that remain as vestiges of wine country history. By 2003, the winery was in a state of disrepair, completely encapsulated in a derelict warehouse structure. Undaunted, the Halls were determined to bring it back to life. Although the building's condition dictated that only key historic elements could be salvaged and preserved, the team carefully documented the details of the existing building and rebuilt it with modern materials and methods to

The Hall Wines campus is replete with intentional juxtapositions:
old and new, rustic and contemporary, hard-edged but softened
by the trees and grasses that surround the structures.

match the original. Since no original drawings remained, they worked from period photographs. The historic stone base remained, but the barn-like structure above was newly constructed by local artisans and stained by hand to look as if it had always been there. Used for special events, it establishes a centerpiece for the campus, honors the heritage of the property, and provides a counterpoint for the strikingly contemporary new winery building.

Hall is not a singular structure, nor is it a singular experience. It is, rather, a carefully curated set of experiences within the landscape and the built environment. The design is replete with intentional juxtapositions: old and new, rustic and contemporary, and hard-edged but softened by the trees and grasses that surround the structures. In fact, the landscape, and the artwork carefully placed with in it, form the connective tissue that binds the buildings together into a cohesive whole.

The journey begins before visitors set foot on the property, when the 35-foot *Bunny Foo Foo,* rendered in polished stainless steel, first comes into view from Highway 29. Designed by Laurence Argent, the sculpture is playful, personal, and entertaining, an immediate indication that Hall has been built for the celebration of both wine and art.

Once visitors arrive, the journey is carefully choreographed. A massive heritage oak tree sits directly on axis with the entry door, connected by a walkway that is tapered ever so slightly to draw visitors toward the entry. Glass entry doors are rimmed in Corten steel, that was left to age to a rough, chalky texture and then are unexpectedly backlit in Hall's signature red. The entry space is small, one of a series of points of tension and release that mark the journey through the architecture. Multiple contemplative spaces become the architectural equivalent of breathing room to take in the artwork.

In direct juxtaposition to the rustic historicism of the Peterson-Bergfeld building, the winery is starkly contemporary—a glass structure composed of two horizontal planes. The roof seems to float in space, but it is actually a 30-foot cantilever, supported by just two columns and free from horizontal beams that might disrupt the sweeping views of the Mayacamas Mountains. This magical illusion is made possible by structural glass fins set perpendicular to the glass that wraps the space.

The lack of elevation changes on the flat site challenged the team to create a sense of elevation within the building itself. By elevating the main tasting area to the second floor and rendering it nearly transparent, the team captured the sweeping views of the vineyards and the mountain range just beyond. Tucked underneath the tasting room, an intimate gathering space for special tastings is enclosed and hushed, opening onto a members-only lower terrace.

Jarrod emphasizes that this project was one of his most deeply collaborative, with architect and artists working hand in hand to create this highly evolved envelope for their art pieces. Each of the dozens of pieces was commissioned specifically for this site, just as the architecture was designed specifically to house the

The view from the production winery, past Jim Campbell's light installation *Exploded View* and through the VIP tasting rooms to the courtyard beyond is the architect's favorite.

ESCORTED TOURS
ONLY

THE LIBRARY

VACA SALON

One of Kathryn Hall's favorite collaborations between architect and artist is in the main tasting room, where artist Spencer Finch's colorful mural and installation of dozens of glass squares both capture and reflect the views visible from Jarrod Denton's glass box.

artwork. Sculptures by Jaume Plensa, John Baldessari, Francois-Xavier Lalanne, Patrick Dougherty, and many others live within the landscape.

One of Kathryn's favorite collaborations between art and architecture is in the main tasting room. To direct the eye to the views beyond the glass walls, Jarrod painted the interior surfaces a dark shade, creating a frame for the views. Artist Spencer Finch conceived a mural for the rear wall that mirrors the colors of the landscape, and he hung dozens of individual glass squares from nearly invisible wires over that tasting bar. Each of the squares moves subtly and independently in the breeze from the open doorways, creating an organic sense of movement in direct contrast to the space's hard edges. Within this glass box, everything illuminates, or reflects, the surroundings. Viewed from the courtyard as the sun sets in late afternoon, the entire western facade becomes a reflection of the landscape.

Jarrod Denton loves an immersive experience, and he is tirelessly attentive to detail. But most telling of all, he thoroughly enjoys returning to his projects to experience every detail. The winery structure is comprised of a series of moments, each one better than the next. On a tour through the building, Jarrod pauses on the landing overlooking the entry to look back at the view of the heritage oak. He declares, "This is my favorite moment," only to override himself with, "No, this is my favorite moment," again and again.

On the mezzanine he stops, looking out at the views framed by the three private tasting rooms that fan out across from the large production area. Set at the center of the winery, these three spaces provide a deeply engaging experience, where visitors can look out to where the grapes are grown, hear and smell the grapes being processed on the adjacent mezzanine, and taste the end product. But though it's close, this is not Jarrod's favorite moment.

He walks through to the glass doors to the mezzanine that floats above the fermentation tanks and says decisively, "This really is my favorite moment, and it's in the production area. The workers share the same access to views and art installations as the visitors and club members do." Constructed to facilitate a gravity-fed process, the double-height production space opens to the through views and is filled with artwork. Graham Caldwell's *Red Rain* and *Pinwheels* by Jim Drain and Ara Peterson hang above the tanks. Jim Campbell's installation, *Exploded View*— comprised of 1,728 LEDs—crosses the glass boundary between the production and hospitality spaces, effectively knitting them together.

The Halls take their hospitality seriously. In early meetings, they had described the ideal winery guests: they stay five hours then have an amazing experience that they take home with them and share with their friends. On a later visit, Jarrod stopped to talk with a group visiting from Tennessee. When he mentioned that he was the architect, the group raved, telling him they had been there for four or five hours, met new friends, and planned to go home and tell all their friends about it. His comment: "They nailed it."

Ray, a host and ambassador at Hall Wines, sums up the experience: "Winemaking takes place in the vineyard; this place is about our personality, about who we are."

The curtain walls allow visitors to walk right up to the glass as if there were no walls at all, a dramatic, if a bit disconcerting, effect.

OPPOSITE ABOVE: *Sanna*, by Jaume Plensa, a larger-than-life head sculpted of marble and steel, keeps watch over the central courtyard.

OPPOSITE BELOW: The 35-foot *Bunny Foo Foo*, rendered in polished stainless steel by artist Laurence Argent, lets visitors know they have arrived.

ABOVE: Originally constructed in 1885, the Peterson-Bergfeld building is one of California's best-known ghost wineries.

The design of Hall Wines was a deeply collaborative effort, with architect and artists working hand in hand to create a home for the wines and the art collection. The result is in equal parts a winery, a museum, and a place to entertain on a grand scale.

CADE ESTATE

STEWARDS OF THEIR ENVIRONMENT

LOCATION: **HOWELL MOUNTAIN** | ARCHITECTURE: **SIGNUM ARCHITECTURE**

Set high atop Napa Valley's Howell Mountain, CADE Estate is the second of three wineries in the PlumpJack Group portfolio of wineries. Partners Gavin Newsom, Gordon Getty, and John Conover make their guiding philosophy of environmental responsibility very clear: "At CADE Estate, we believe that winemaking should honor the land, both aesthetically and environmentally."

CADE Estate has the distinction of being just the second LEED Gold-certified winery in the Napa Valley. While building a LEED Gold-certified winery was initially Gavin Newsom's idea, his business partners were quick to agree. "We are stewards of our environment," insists John Conover, partner and general manager of the group's three wineries. "We are just passing through, but what we build is not."

Looking for a complement to their first winery, the group purchased the fifty-four-acre property that would become CADE Estate in 2005. At 1,800 feet, the steeply sloped site was set high above the fog line, with unparalleled views of the valley. The group needed an architect who shared their environmental ideals, and who would take risks to carry out their bold vision.

As is so often the case in the wine country, the group found their architect through a trust-

ed friend. Builder Mark Grassi, who was already on board to build the yet-to-be designed winery, introduced them to Juancarlos Fernandez of newly established St. Helena-based Signum Architecture. Juancarlos had never designed a winery but had already built a reputation as a brilliant architect. Tending toward minimalism, his design philosophy combines a sustainable sensibility with an attention to detail and propensity for thinking outside the box that proved to be the perfect fit for the PlumpJack Group.

John Conover is quick to sing his architect's praises. "You know when you meet someone and there is an instant connection? That was Juancarlos." He trusted him implicitly to take risks and carry out the group's vision. When asked to describe his feelings about the project, Juancarlos is succinct and to the point. "It is one of the great joys of my career. Of all of the projects I've taken on, this is absolutely my favorite."

The design brief was driven by two core doctrines: design sustainably and treat every decision as an opportunity to do something different. Juancarlos added a third: create a sense of discovery.

The experience at CADE begins with the steep, winding driveway carved from an existing logging road. As the road curves around on itself, the solid form of the production building comes into view. The concrete, glass, and steel structure speaks directly to the masculinity of Howell Mountain and the muscular nature of the wines produced there. The winery's many vertical elements commune with the large fir trees that surround it. The inverted roofline hides solar arrays and white roofs that reflect the sun's heat and contribute to the building's LEED Gold rating.

In contrast to the production building, the hospitality building remains hidden, tucked nearly out of view. Visitors are directed down a discreet walkway, their view of what lies ahead intentionally blocked by a freestanding wall until they round a corner and come face-to-face with one of the most dramatic views in the Napa Valley. Juancarlos points out the tension created when the space closes in and then opens up to reveal the full scope of the view, intensifying the experience.

Juancarlos calls the production and hospitality spaces "brother and sister buildings," related in design and materials, but set apart by their varied scale. The journey through and between these sibling structures is attenuated. After entering through the portal into the transformative experience on the terrace, visitors soak in the immersive experience of wine, architecture, and views. A decomposed granite walkway winds around the hospitality structure and up past the views of the adjacent vineyards to the production building.

The large winery production building was carefully placed to fit between the existing trees. The team proudly points out that only two trees were removed to construct the entire building and, as Juancarlos describes it, "one was dead, and one was a leaner." The curved wall that defines the entry to the production building was designed as a direct response to the natural bowl that cradles the winery.

The buildings are comprised of weighty masses, but the attention to detail is extraordinary if subtle. Every architectural decision had a functional purpose and every choice conveys meaning. Craftsmanship that might have been overlooked is brought to the foreground to be acknowledged and admired. Door openings in the concrete walls are saw-cut to show the patterns of the aggregate within. Board-formed concrete wainscoting creates a subtle change of texture at eye level and is echoed in the board-formed patterning on the steel cave doors.

The team wanted to leave the land as they found it, with minimal human intervention. Materials were chosen to age in place, taking up residence alongside the rocks, oaks, and manzanitas that populate the hillsides. Textured concrete provides heft and Alaskan Red Cedar has aged to meet the weathered palette of its surroundings. There is no manicured landscape; the site was hydroseeded with exactly what had existed before construction commenced. Only the manzanitas planted along the curved concrete wall, native to these hillsides, were brought in.

Since they were at the forefront sustainable winery design, Juancarlos invented the approach as he went along. As one LEED inspector pointed out on a visit to the construction site, it was important that CADE succeed in order to provide an example to others that a winery could be designed and constructed to exacting LEED standards.

PREVIOUS OVERLEAF: The unique shape of the cave walls, with their oval portals and overlapping ceiling planes, faintly echoes the shape of the shield that forms the distinctive PlumpJack Group logo.

ABOVE: The industrial nature of the materials, chosen to age in place, speaks directly to the rugged mountain site.

On the tasting terrace, visitors soak in the immersive experience of wine, architecture, and views.

Juancarlos was adamant that production function not be sacrificed to create a showcase, and John agreed. Function is paramount, and beauty grows from the efficiency with which each design element fulfills its purpose. Vertical bands of structural glass let in light and, along with rooftop solar panels, minimize energy usage. Massive concrete walls hide water tanks and provide passive cooling in the non-conditioned winery. Trex, used throughout the production facility, insures against mold and rot and decreases the number of trees used in construction. Recycled materials used throughout both buildings minimize the winery's ecological impact.

Every design decision conveys meaning, though that meaning is sometimes hidden from view. The unique shape of the cave walls, with their oval portals and overlapping ceiling planes, faintly echoes the shape of the shield that forms the distinctive PlumpJack Group logo. Of course, most will not notice this, but it's there nonetheless, part of the ethos of the place.

OPPOSITE: The diminutive hospitality building shows a solid front upon approach, so visitors experience the full force of the view only as they step through the threshold.

ABOVE: A line of posts creates a play of light and shadow on the entry wall.

ABOVE: Drains, a necessary element of every production winery, are tucked under concrete tanks set on platforms cantilevered out over the production floor, keeping the floor seamless and clear for work.

OPPOSITE: The production winery's massive steel door pivots in a circle, echoing the oculus in the overhang above.

The inverted roofline of the production winery removes the roof element that typically makes up a third of a building's architectural proportions, reducing its visual impact on the site.

LAW ESTATE WINES

CONTEMPORARY DESIGN WITH A WARM WELCOME

LOCATION: **PASO ROBLES** | ARCHITECTURE: **BAR ARCHITECTS**

Like many successful endeavors, Don and Susie Law's wine adventure has been a blend of serendipity and determination.

When the Denver-based couple started looking for property in California in 2006, they focused on California's central coast, looking at sites from Monterey to Santa Barbara. Aware that Bill and Liz Armstrong, friends from Denver and owners of nearby Epoch Estate Wines, had settled in Paso Robles, Don and Susie fell in love with it as well.

Don and Susie searched for two years to find the right land to plant what they wanted—Rhone varietals, particularly Syrah, Grenache, and Mourvedre. What they needed were steep slopes and a high elevation with dry, difficult, calcareous land. As a geotechnical engineer, Don knows a thing or two about soil. In his words, "Crappy soil makes great wine."

They assembled their estate in stages, starting with the hillside directly across from the ridge where the winery now sits. Before purchasing the land, they drilled forty-two pits to test the soil. It was pure limestone. Wasting no time, they purchased the land in 2007 and planted their first vines in 2008. Now all they needed was land for a winery.

Then came the second stroke of luck. At just about the same time the Laws started looking for a site for their new winery, a neighbor decided to sell his land. As luck would have it, the land was located just across the road from the Law's new vineyard—60 acres of steeply rolling hillsides and a ridgeline with views for miles. Don's reaction to Ted's offer to sell him the land was, "Give me a number." Ted gave it to him, and the land changed hands. Almost immediately they were up walking the ridge, envisioning their winery. "My favorite part of the process was the dreaming," Susie recalls.

Then came the third happenstance. Although BAR Architects has a long history in San Francisco and a strong reputation for winery design, they somehow did not find their way onto Don and Susie's initial list of designers. Then came the call from BAR principal Jeff Goodwin, who had read about the project on Susie's blog. He told them simply, "We'd really like to work on your project." Impressed, they arranged to meet, and BAR quickly became the obvious choice.

Don and Susie knew they wanted to do something that was new to Paso Robles. They wanted a contemporary design that was all about the views, but not a cold glass box. "One of the best things about Paso Robles is that everyone feels that a rising tide lifts all boats," says Susie. "It's a small community where everyone helps one another and we celebrate each other's successes." They wanted their winery to express the warmth and welcome they felt in their adopted Paso Robles community.

The goals were clear from the start: contemporary architecture, warm and residential interiors, sustainable approach to design, and a celebration of their spectacular location. Susie's initial gut feeling proved true. The synergy and trust between client and architect allowed the Laws to give Jeff and his team a great deal of creative freedom. Jeff knew that with this winery, Don and Susie were establishing their place as involved members of the Paso Robles community. However, that creative freedom did not mean the couple was hands-off. Don and Susie, along with their winemaker, Scott Hawley, were involved every step of the way and attended every entitlement meeting.

Minimal intervention was their mantra—views, site and grapes should all be kept as intact as possible. The winery sits just below the spine of the ridge, shielded from view as visitors approach along Peachy Canyon Road. Yet it is set just high enough to preserve views over the ridgeline and back toward the vineyards on the opposite hillside to the north. The overall effect is extraordinary, and the abundance of glass provides views for miles. "You almost feel as if you can see the ocean in the distance, though, of course, you can't," Jeff says.

The building is immediately impressive. A massive wall of Corten steel punctured by a concrete spine running through the center of the primary east-west axis forms a monolithic structure, while the concrete spine, set askew, provides visual tension. The expanses of Corten steel, board-formed concrete, and Douglas fir give the contemporary structure an earthy quality. The rough outlines of the board-formed concrete counter the sleek outlines of the glass expanses.

At Law Estate Wines, the grapes are organically farmed and processed with as little mechanical intervention as possible. The winery is designed with gravity flow, and, in keeping with the Law's commitment to sustainability, butterfly roofs over the production facility collect rainwater. An angled shed roof with expansive overhangs floods the interior with as much northern light as possible while shading the outdoor terraces. Solar panels capture energy from the Paso Robles sunshine, and generous light from windows in the fermentation building alleviate the need for electrical lighting. A bioreactor captures wastewater, processes the waste, and then sends it to irrigation tanks to water the vineyards. Xeriscape landscape by San Francisco–based Lutsko Associates minimizes water use.

The Laws were pioneers of sorts, the first in Paso Robles to hold tastings by appointment only so that visitors felt like invited guests. They were the first to conduct their tastings as flights: guests move through the wines at their leisure, comparing and contrasting as they go, and each group that visits the winery has its own staff member. Visiting the winery is very much like hanging out in a friend's living room. There is no tasting bar, just a long dining table, a comfortable arrangement of sofas, and wraparound terraces with abundant seating for guests who want to stick around and enjoy the view.

"We want them to stay awhile," says Susie with a smile.

PREVIOUS OVERLEAF: A massive wall of Corten steel forms a monolithic structure, set against xeriscape landscape by Lutsko Associates.

ABOVE: The design goals were clear: contemporary architecture, warm and residential interiors, and a sustainable approach to design.

The winery sits just below the spine of the ridge, shielded from view, yet it is set just high enough to preserve views over the ridgeline and back toward the vineyards on the opposite hillside to the north.

ABOVE: The expanses of Corten steel, board-formed concrete, and Douglas fir give the contemporary structure an earthy quality.

OPPOSITE: A dramatically angled shed roof with expansive overhangs floods the interior with as much northern light as possible while shading the outdoor terraces.

Visiting the winery is like visiting the home of friends—the experience is casual and inviting. The Laws want their visitors to relax and stay awhile.

HAMEL
FAMILY WINES

A FAMILY AFFAIR

LOCATION: **SONOMA VALLEY** | ARCHITECTURE: **GOULD EVANS**

If you were to choose a single word to describe George Hamel it would have to be "effusive." The cofounder (with his wife Pam) and patriarch of Hamel Family Wines is not shy about sharing his enthusiasm—for his wine, his family, his architect, his county, his alma mater, or his ideals—and it's infectious.

When George and Pam first purchased a home in Kenwood, in the heart of Sonoma County, they had no plans to get into the wine business. Then their son John started working with Worldwide Opportunities on Organic Farms (WWOOF), an organization dedicated to promoting educational exchange and organic farming around the world. In a bit of serendipity, John was assigned to a farm in the Napa Valley, just over the Mayacamas Mountains from Kenwood. He immersed himself in the agricultural bounty of California's wine country, and it wasn't long before his family was drawn in as well.

When the Hamels banded together to form Hamel Family Wines, it was truly a family affair. Two of George's four children signed on to work with him in the business. John is the winemaker, collaborating with consultant Martha McClellan, and his brother George III (known to nearly everyone as "GIII") runs the front of house as the general manager. "George just loves working with his sons," says Pam. "Not a lot of families can do it, but the Hamel family can."

In 2010, the Hamels purchased what is now called Hamel Family Ranch, a 125-acre parcel of gentle slopes at the base of the Mayacama Mountain Range, very near the center of the Sonoma Valley AVA. Once owned by William Randolph Hearst, the land lies just uphill from Highway 12, which traverses the Sonoma Valley and acts as its quintessential wine road. Yet the road might as well be a million miles away. Guests seated on the winery's expansive patio overlooking the sloping vineyards can neither see nor hear it.

When it came time to build the winery, the family started from scratch. As the younger George puts it, "My family doesn't have the sexy story of being fifth-generation grape growers or fifth-generation winemakers, but we've made a commitment to quality, starting in the vineyard, going into the winery, and then curating a quality experience that's unlike any other in Sonoma Valley or anywhere in Northern California." They had never made wine or built a winery, but they were very clear about the experience they wanted to create.

George is effusive in his passion for the wine business, and he is equally effusive in his praise for his architect. "We started out with an architectural beauty contest of sorts, but we didn't want to just round up the usual suspects," he declares. "When we interviewed Doug, the connection was immediate."

Since the Hamels were new to the wine business, Douglas Thornley and his team at Gould Evans started with a site study and programming session to help the family think through the wine-making process. He talked with them about what kind of experience they would like to create, explaining that the architecture was an envelope for that experience. He listened carefully to their priorities—sustainability, privacy, and hospitality. The team roamed the site in an ATV (which Douglas insists is one of the best perks of designing a winery), with Douglas's wife, Susan, snapping photographs of the site from every angle and vantage point.

George laughs when he talks about their first meeting. "Doug met with us, listened to everything we had to say, and then completely ignored us!" Then he adds, "Thank goodness he did, or we would have ended up with a French château."

He is only half joking. Though the family had come to the design team with photographs of traditional old-world wineries, Douglas knew that the kind of experience they were looking for—connected to the land, sustainably constructed, immersed in the views, flexible and adaptable for a range of events with a free flow between indoors and out—called for a more contemporary architectural solution. Call it a traditional soul expressed through contemporary architecture.

When Pam was not entirely convinced, Douglas and his team constructed an architectural model. Douglas placed the model into the ATV, drove them all to the site they had chosen for the winery, and set it on the hood. He then asked Pam to look through the openings that would eventually become expanses of glass framing the views. She did, and from that point on, they were all in.

Douglas cites his experience studying architecture in Denmark—living amongst Danish architects and training at the Royal Academy of Art in Copenhagen—as a pivotal point in the development of his approach to design. Indeed, there is a certain lightness of being to each of his projects, clearly informed by the simplicity, purity, and elegance of Danish design.

The winery's hospitality building—the Hamels call it the Estate House—cantilevers over the vineyard, floating like a transparent jewel box over the sloping site. Continuous clerestory windows allow the roof to float above the tasting room walls. Inside and out, walls painted a soft green somehow seem to disappear and broad expanses of glass invite the greens and golds of the hillside deep into the building. The building's subtle hues allow the experience to be defined by the

PREVIOUS OVERLEAF: The oak tree that anchors the eastern corner of the tasting room is so integral to the design it seems part of the building itself.

ABOVE: The Estate House cantilevers out—a transparent jewel box floating over the adjacent vineyard.

The layout of the winery is flexible and adaptable for a range of events, with a free flow from indoors and out.

ABOVE: The colors of the surrounding environment are reflected in the building's materials, while broad expanses of glass bring hues of the surrounding vineyard into the interior.

OPPOSITE: An opening in the 125-foot rammed-earth wall provides a perfect view of the terrace and vineyards.

The end of each of the cave's three bores is left unfinished to illustrate the unique qualities of the soil.

shapes and colors seen through the glass. The majestic existing oak that anchors the eastern corner is so integral to the interior experience that it seems almost a part of the building itself.

An impressive pair of 125-foot rammed-earth walls running the length of the hospitality building acts as its defining principle, their striated patterns a reflection of the golden hills and corduroy patterns of the vineyard rows. The pattern is, in turn, picked up by the marbling of the travertine tasting bar and fireplace. Aligned in both style and purpose, the architectural elements all speak to one another, but they do so softly.

The Hamel Family ranch and vineyards are farmed biodynamically. Everything used in the wine-making process stays on the property, reused and redistributed for another use in what George calls "a recurring cycle of life that makes the wines distinctive and uniquely of the place." From the beginning, everyone agreed that the winery should be designed as a single entity with production, hospitality, and caves grouped together as a holistic unit, and that the winery should be constructed using the most sustainable methods available. Although they elected not to pursue formal certification, the design team used LEED Platinum principles as a benchmark.

The Hamels worked with Douglas to choose sustainable materials: FSC-certified wood throughout, a living roof atop the production facility for natural insulation, and retaining walls rendered in pisé mixed with earth from the caves. Basalt pavers that cover the floor inside and out transition from a grouted interior installation to a floating system on the outdoor patio, which, with its lack of grouting, creates a permeable surface. And then there are those monumental rammed-earth walls, created with the help of the late David Easton, considered by many to be the grandfather of rammed earth.

The 12,000 square feet of caves cut into the hillside provided the material for the winery's signature rammed-earth walls and contributed to the retaining walls. Lined with sand from Monterey Bay, the caves also host the winery's VIP tasting experience. A small reserve tasting room is set at a strategically placed bend in the cave. The "wiggle" was Douglas's idea. "It inserts a sense of mystery," he says. "You don't have a sense of how big the caves are, so you have to discover it for yourself." The reserve tasting room is insulated and closed off from the caves, which have notoriously poor acoustics. A round table sits at the center of the perfectly symmetrical space, topped by a barrel-vaulted ceiling that allows even the faintest whisper to be heard on the other side of the room.

Although they have been approved for eventual production of 30,000 cases, the Hamels have chosen to build only 12,000 square feet of caves so far, electing to build production and cave space up to their potential over time. In the meantime, a tour of the caves comes with an unexpected bonus. A view of exposed earth at the end of each of the three bores—each completely different in tone—is a vivid expression of the individual characteristics of the land, and a peek into what makes this place so special.

SINGULAR
VOICES

STEWART CELLARS

A CALIFORNIA AESTHETIC WITH A EUROPEAN SENSE OF PLACE

LOCATION: **YOUNTVILLE**

ARCHITECTURE: **ARCANUM ARCHITECTURE**

Located in the heart of the Napa Valley, Yountville is almost impossibly picturesque. Walkable, friendly, and home to some of the most venerated restaurants in the country, this small town has become a mecca for food, wine, and hospitality. A small-town sense of community mingles with heightened culinary sensibilities to create an air of magic.

James Stewart, who opened Stewart Cellars in downtown Yountville in 2016, is well aware of his role in this magical place. "Yountville sets the bar high in terms of the culinary and hospitality experience. We were very conscious of that bar and we wanted to exceed it." It was important to the Stewarts to fit into the fabric of their new community and make a positive impact on the town.

To achieve those goals, James hired Anthony Fish of Arcanum Architects to design what would be the firm's second winery project. "I looked at a lot of architects," says James. "For me, Anthony brought together a combination of historic sensibility and a modern outlook that was very expressive of California." James and Anthony are clearly friends, and the success of the space derives from the trust they have in one another.

Founder Michael Stewart, James's father, began making wine as a hobby but the effort quickly became a family collaboration. When James joined the business in 2005, the winery was producing 800 cases a year. Not a group to do things halfway, the family hired Paul Hobbs, whom James calls the "Steve Jobs of wine," as consulting winemaker. Stewart Cellars is now a full family affair. James's brother-in-law, Blair Guthrie, is the winemaker, and sister, Caroline Stewart Guthrie, who trained with Paul Hobbs in Argentina and has a natural talent for wine, runs day-to-day operations and "holds it all together." James regards it as his job to give roots to the operation, take the long view, and establish it firmly for generations to come. Vintners are renowned for taking the long view, and this family is no exception.

Prior to establishing this foothold in Yountville, the Stewart wine-making operation had no public presence. James made numerous scouting trips from his residence in San Francisco, searching for the perfect home—one that fit the family's vision for Stewart Cellars—for the winery's new hospitality space. On one such trip, as James sat eating lunch at chef Richard Reddington's Redd Wood, he looked out at Grady's Garage across the street. Old and showing its age, the garage had been there forever. It was one of the few underdeveloped parcels left on the town's picturesque main street. Inspired, James cold-called the owner to see if he would sell, never expecting him to accept the offer. But he did.

Together, James and Anthony explored the idea of what an in-town winery hospitality experience should be. The town's planning codes limited the individual structures to 5,000 square feet each, and a combination of uses was important to the city. This fit the family's vision perfectly: a collection of intimate spaces built around a series of three courtyards—a diminutive entry courtyard with seating for the small dining space, a large interior courtyard set between the tasting barn and the Nomad Heritage Library, and a third courtyard centered around an expansive heritage oak tree they went to great lengths to save.

The three structures surround the interior courtyard, a casual and flexible space that can be configured in any number of ways for various events and gatherings. At the front of the property a semitransparent structure acts as a vestibule of sorts, housing the popular Southside Cafe. Flanking the central courtyard, the Nomad Heritage Library and Tasting Hall are highly individual spaces, personal and welcoming. It all comes together in a California aesthetic but with a very European sense of place.

Stewart Cellars is also European in its layered sense of history and imagination. "I wanted to transport people into an environment that tells a story," asserts James. Inspired by the Stewart family's Scottish roots and the intersection of old and new, the team built both the story and the structures around the winery's massive stone walls. Gleaning their inspiration from ancient stone relics scattered throughout Scotland, the team envisioned a winery rebuilt within the ancient stone walls of an old Scottish abbey.

Although Stewart Cellars is entirely new construction, the layering of materials—raked cedar walls set within with stone walls that bookend the Nomad Heritage Library for instance—define an experience similarly layered over time, an ancient structure repurposed for contemporary use.

Built of local Syre stone, which is only found in the Napa Valley, the walls tell a local story as well. Though it's an in-town winery, Stewart Cellars is very much of the land and place. The masonry work was critical to the team's vision. Door and window openings were saw-cut to look as if they were hewn from the existing walls, and the stone coursing had to be perfectly imperfect to render the sense of agrarian history the team was striving for. Stone courses run right up to the edges of the clean-lined steel doors and windows, without the usual stone framework, and the steel frames are set into notches cut into the stone to hide their sleek edges.

"We had the stone taken off and reset three times," jokes James. "Our contractor had the patience of a saint." General contractors Jim Murphy & Associates are well known in the wine country for their exacting attention to detail, and the stone masons at Shannon Masonry are highly skilled at their craft.

James's personality comes through in every element of the design. He worked with interior designer Ken Fulk to create collected, curated spaces that reflect his diverse interests and passions. The Nomad Heritage Library, a cozy, almost moody

PREVIOUS OVERLEAF: In a nod to the family's Scottish heritage, the story of Stewart Cellars centers on the stone walls inspired by the stone relics scattered across the Scottish landscape.

ABOVE: Stewart Cellars is a collection of small-scale buildings surrounding a series of courtyards of varying scale.

It was important to the Stewarts that their new in-town hospitality center fit into the fabric of their new community and make a positive impact on the town. The diminutive restaurant at the front of the site acts as the property's front door.

LEFT: The Nomad Library, open to wine club members, is a quirky, curated space filled with books and a rotating collection of curiosities.

OPPOSITE: Every element of the design tells a story. The slim steel rods that line the Tasting Hall bar visually reference James Stewart's other wine label, Quell.

space that feels as if it has been there forever, speaks volumes about his personal vision and interests. True to its name, it is filled with books—all for sale—along with a continuously evolving collection of curiosities. James's obsession with science fiction is evident throughout, but the book collection is wide ranging and ever changing. This collection includes favorites from the entire family, including wine education, great reads, fashion, art, and architecture. Visitors can pick up books that range from the recently published *Women of the Napa Valley* to a copy of Ayn Rand's *Atlas Shrugged* or George Orwell's classic *1984*.

The Tasting Hall's bar, custom made by Concreteworks, is scored with slim steel rods. The rods, which start out separated and a bit chaotic and then subtly align to form a tightly aligned pattern as they travel the length of the bar, echo the design of James Stewart's own label, Quell.

In this assemblage of structure and spaces, contrast is important. Just as the contemporary materials and modern farmhouse vernacular contrast with the rough-hewn stone walls with their air of age, the quirky, collected nature of designer Ken Fulk's interiors provide a lively sense of contrast to the architecture. The indoor-outdoor spaces provide a direct connection to the landscape and the changing seasons.

Above all, Stewart Cellars beckons to the many who walk the town's lovely main street. "We were surprised by the amount of families we attracted," remarks James. "Your customers tell you what your place is going to be. It's important to have a vision, but then you need to be able to adapt and add to that vision as you go along. That's how your customers become part of your story."

THE DONUM ESTATE

A GIFT FROM THE LAND

LOCATION: **CARNEROS** | ARCHITECTURE: **MATT HOLLIS ARCHITECTS**

Carneros occupies a unique place in the California wine country. Cooled by bayfront breezes, it's where Sonoma County touches the San Francisco Bay. This is Pinot Noir country, and home to the Donum Estate.

Anne Moller-Racke's history on this land spans decades, and this is where her heart lies. She came to Sonoma County in 1981 from her native Germany to help run Buena Vista Winery. During her early years in California, she trained with industry icons such as Andre Tchelistcheff, and she was later instrumental in establishing Carneros as an AVA. When she became Buena Vista's vice president of vineyard operations in the early 1990s, she managed land that included what is now the Donum Estate, and she planted its original vines in 1997. When the Moller-Racke family sold Buena Vista in 2001, they retained the Carneros vineyards and renamed the property the Donum Estate. This would become Anne's project and her life's work.

Ten years later, when the family sold the Donum Estate, Anne stayed on as president and winegrower, remaining inextricably connected to the land, but now with the freedom and capital to expand and improve it. The new ownership group had visited and fallen in love with the Donum

Estate wines, and Anne's Burgundian approach to winemaking—the concept of estate, tending small individual blocks, and attending to the details of the land. Devoted to the quality and integrity of the land, the new partners kept the mission of the Donum Estate intact. It is, according to Anne, a seamless and supportive partnership.

Allan and Mei Warburg, today's owners, worked with Anne and a vineyard team to carefully study how to best develop the land. They had fallen in love with the authentic, rural nature of this former dairy farm, and it was important to them that they honor the land's roots. They hired Matt Hollis, founder of San Francisco–based Matt Hollis Architects, to carry out their vision.

They wanted to celebrate what they call "the important connection between art, nature, and the human hand." The Donum Estate would soon house not only a new winery and hospitality center, but an astounding sculpture collection. Since 2015, Allan and his wife have built a collection of forty large-scale sculptures, which have been installed one by one amid the vineyard landscape. An eclectic mix of contemporary work by both established and emerging artists from the East and West— including Ai Weiwei, Keith Haring, Jaume Plensa,

PREVIOUS OVERLEAF: A row of skylights is met by the sinuous curve of the opposing roofline in the hospitality building.

ABOVE: Matt Hollis and his team played with the Sonoma farmhouse aesthetic—simple white structures with board-and-batten siding—to create an architectural vocabulary that is fresh and new.

Louise Bourgeois, and many others—is quite possibly the largest collection of world-class art ever assembled in a vineyard setting. The growing sculpture collection and the design for the new hospitality center and winery developed hand in hand, a symbiosis that forms the heart and soul of the project. "Allan and Mei are creating something that they expect to own in perpetuity," says architect Matt Hollis.

Sonoma County is dairy country, and the history of agricultural structures runs deep here. Matt's design for the Donum Estate honors the legacy of the dairy that once occupied the site. His strategy was to create a dispersed set of structures—a collected grouping that tell the story of generations of use—much like you would find on a working dairy or farm. The winery (still under construction as of this writing) sits on land that was once the dairy barn. The former milking shed has been refurbished and is now used to house the property's numerous animals. An original caretaker's house, with its traditional white clapboard siding renovated and preserved, provides the inspiration for the hospitality building's contemporary take on the farmhouse vernacular. The new hospitality building occupies the site of the former farmhouse, capitalizing upon the best views of the rolling, vineyard-covered hills, adjacent wetlands, and San Francisco Bay in the distance.

Traditionally, farmhouse structures in Sonoma County are comprised of white gabled buildings with board and batten siding. Matt and his team matched that aesthetic, then played with it to create an architectural vocabulary that is fresh and new but grounded in local vernacular. The footprint of the hospitality building is straightforward: a simple peaked roof flanked by flat-roofed sections on either side. Matt clad the building in board-and-batten siding but tweaked the formula, playing with the width and spacing of the battens to lend dimension to the flat planes and a bit of irreverence to the all-white structure. Matt describes the plays on pattern and perception as a kind of topographical map, in which the increasing and decreasing spacing of the lines tell the story of the land's contours.

The clean, white forms create a pristine backdrop for the contemporary art collection. The interplay between architecture and art is immediate. *Pumpkin*, by artist Yayoi Kasuma, rests upon a plinth at the center of a fountain simply wrought from local stone, quietly marking the entry to the tasting experience. Set within a slim concrete portal, 10-foot copper entry doors were treated to speed up the oxidation process that would have happened over time, rendering them a striking shade of blue-green. The team considered glass entry doors but preferred the solid doors for their sense of mystery and arrival.

The hospitality building interior is clean and spare. Clothed in all white walls, minimal trim, and wide plank white oak floors, the aesthetic is distinctly Danish. The central great room is flanked by a matched pair of tasting rooms. Glass doors slide back to render the demarcation between indoors and out nearly transparent, and barn doors on the interior slide silently closed to create a private tasting experience in which each group feels alone with the land.

Board-and-batten siding in a variety of widths lends a bit of irreverence to the simple farmhouse shapes.

OPPOSITE ABOVE: The deceptively simple structure created to house the iron prototype of Louise Bourgeois's *Crouching Spider*, provides the spider with a breathtaking view of the vineyards and bay.

OPPOSITE BELOW: The simplicity of the dispersed white structures creates an effective backdrop for the collection of artwork installed throughout the estate; a statue by Jaume Plensa greets visitors upon arrival.

ABOVE: Louise Bourgeois's *Crouching Spider* is a prototype for the artist's well-known collection of large-scale spiders, which includes a giant installation at the Tate Modern in London.

Within the great room, five large skylights line the north vault of the gable. With the skylights lining the north side, the question became, "Well, what do we do with the south side?" Introduce a curve, of course. The sinuous curve set across from the skylights allows the light to rake across the ceiling in dramatic fashion.

With the exception of the gable, ceiling heights were designed at 10 feet. But just as the foundations were being poured, Allan procured a painting for the tasting area that measured 10 feet square. In a flurry, the team redesigned the proportions to accommodate 11-foot ceiling heights, allowing the new acquisition the space it needed to occupy the great room. As a result, the vertical window sections became more attenuated, lightening the proportions in a way the team could not have envisioned. Exterior awnings, inspired by traditional farm fencing, play with proportion, bulky yet somehow feminine, reinforced by the new height and more delicate proportions of the windows.

A simple pavilion sits in the vineyards in view of the hospitality building. In this diminutive, contemporary structure, the team once again played with the proportions of the battens so that they seem to recede toward a central vanishing point. In concert with the large-scale sculptures carefully sited throughout the property, it looks right at home in its spot in the vineyards.

The final building in the collection is a deceptively simple structure just large enough to house a prototype for Louise Bourgeois's *Crouching Spider* series, which, crafted of iron, required a conditioned space. Composed of a solid wall and simple doorway, the entry facade belies the light-filled interior that lies within, reinforcing the sense of discovery and providing the spider with a breathtaking view of the vineyards and bay.

"Magical" is a word that Anne uses repeatedly when she talks about the land she has cultivated for over twenty years. These 200 acres are indeed magical, encompassing rolling hillsides, stands of trees, a large and very picturesque pond surrounded by reeds, and riparian wetlands leading to the Pablo Bay. The landscape is alive and busy, with animals, beehives, an organic farm, and 150-year-old olive trees. Art, nature, wine, and food exist side by side, each enhancing the other.

Anne is entirely at home on the land and in her new role as not only cultivator of the vines but caretaker for the new winery and sculpture collection. "I love the art because it draws people out into the vineyard," she says. She points out that the name *donum* comes from the Latin word for gift. For Anne and the owners, the Donum Estate is a gift from the land.

The clean lines of the interiors evoke a soothing
Scandinavian aesthetic.

WILLIAMS SELYEM WINERY

A TEMPLE TO PINOT NOIR

LOCATION: **HEALDSBURG** | ARCHITECTURE: **ALEX CEPPI, D.ARC GROUP**

The Russian River Valley winds its way north to south through the geographical heart of Sonoma County, curving gently westward on its journey to the Pacific Ocean. The river, as well as proximity to the ocean's cooling breezes, makes this valley prime land for growing cool-climate varietals, particularly Pinot Noir and Chardonnay.

Actually, the Russian River Valley doesn't seem like a single valley at all. It feels more like a series of secret vales, each filled with its own rows of green vineyards. West Side Road, which commences in the wine country town of Healdsburg, hews close to the Russian River. A drive along this country road reveals a glimpse of new valley around every bend, creating a sense of continual discovery.

Williams Selyem sits on the crest of the hill just as the West Side Road and the river it follows makes their most dramatic turn toward the Pacific. The result of this fortuitous location is that the river curves around the winery and vineyards on three sides. Embraced by the river, and set back from the road, the winery seems to sit completely alone in this corner of the world. It was just that singularity of place that drew its owners, John and Kathe Dyson, to purchase it to create the first official home for Williams Selyem wines.

When John and Kathe purchased Williams Selyem in 1998 from its founders, Burt Williams and Ed Selyem, the winery had developed an iconic status within the industry, but it lacked an estate. Burt and Ed had started making wine as a hobby in a garage in nearby Forestville in 1979. In the ensuing years, the duo garnered a sweepstakes prize (for the best red wine) at the California State Fair and a perfect 100-point score from *Wine Enthusiast*; they saw their wine served at the White House and developed a years-long wait just to earn a coveted spot on their allocation list. The Dysons, who also own a winery in New York, had themselves been on the Williams Selyem list.

After purchasing Williams Selyem, John set out to create a home for the storied brand. He did so with a singularity of purpose: to integrate past and future in a single sweeping gesture. He dedicated himself to maintaining the legacy of the founders and expressing their natural and minimal approach to winemaking while simultaneously expressing the brand's iconic status and Sonoma County's cultural evolution.

When John found the property that would become the Williams Selyem estate, it wasn't for sale, and no one knew who owned it. Not easily

PREVIOUS OVERLEAF: Williams Selyem, which is quite unlike anything else in the wine country, speaks its own architectural language derived from its owner's reverence for wine.

ABOVE: The winery is inspired by the shape of the wine barrels, but the owner and architect also wanted to capture the passion, style, and meticulous attention to detail that goes into the making of their Pinot Noir.

deterred, John searched through county records and finally found that the property belonged to Luella Litton, who, it turned out, had passed away, leaving her property to family in Texas. It took John three long years to convince the family to sell. As a tribute to Luella, the Dysons called the property Litton Estate for several years. When the name proved too similar to nearby Lytton Springs Vineyard, they changed it to Williams Selyem Estate; but not wanting to let go of the history, they created Luella's Garden, located just inside the main gate, as a tribute.

It is safe to say that the design of Williams Selyem is unlike anything else in the wine country. It speaks its own architectural language—a language of reverence for the process of turning grapes into wine and for the rich history that precedes it. Inspired by the estates of Bordeaux, which feel like temples to wine, John set out to create a similar expression. He worked with a number of architects as he refined his vision, all along engaging Venezuelan architect Alex Ceppi, of D.arc Group in New York, as a consultant and a sounding board.

"The winery was designed as a temple to Pinot Noir," says John. "No one had used the concept of the barrel as architectural inspiration. That was the vision for the winery. More important, perhaps, was our goal of building a winery that expresses in its form and beauty the effort, passion, attention to detail, and style that goes into the wine itself."

Alex Ceppi had never designed a winery. That didn't worry John, who in the end hired him anyway. Together they sat down to sketch out their thoughts. Displayed on the walls of the production area, those initial sketches look remarkably similar to the final design, a sure sign that the two shared a clear and distilled vision for the project.

The winery's visual impact is immediate and just a little imposing, as a temple to winemaking would logically be. The stairway leading to the main entrance is attenuated, its long, shallow steps forcing visitors to slow down and soak in the building's commanding presence. Though inspired by estates in Bordeaux, the structure is unabashedly contemporary. An ode to the wine-making process, the building is in essence a deconstructed wine barrel with a soaring split-barrel roofline. Entering the winery feels a bit like walking into the center of the barrel itself. A barrel wall backed by clear glass has become the structure's signature element, glowing like a beacon at dusk and leaving just the faintest impression of a stained glass window.

Comprised of soaring spaces and an abundance of light, the building's interior leaves its impact a bit more subtly. Throughout the winery, the palette speaks to the materials of the winemaker's craft: stone, wood, barrel staves, reclaimed

A broad rear terrace provides ample space to host wine club events and presents a unique view of the arching roofline.

A wall of barrels sits directly behind an expanse of glass, creating a dramatic, semitransparent front facade that glows with light in the evening.

vineyard stakes, and just enough white leather on the walls and upholstery to impart elegance and absorb sound. Set within custom-designed glass bricks, a wall of bottles displays every single vintage Williams Selyem has ever produced.

The deeply hued redwood surrounding the entry portal provides a contrast to the lighter tones elsewhere and, like so many of the design details, comes with a story. Long ago, John had come upon old redwood barrels destined for the burn pile at Almaden Winery and, unable to stomach the waste of the precious wood —or the wine-making history it represented—he took the old barrels home, storing them for years until they found their new purpose at the new winery's entrance.

Large valley oaks spread themselves out along the edges of three vast patios, each providing a different view of the tasting room and the vineyards spread out in every direction. Huge boulders are strewn about, looking carefully placed, but in fact were meticulously avoided during construction. The landscape is left largely in its natural state, native and drought resistant. Here again, John was hands on, poring over plant encyclopedias to come up with just the right palette of plant-ings. Two fledgling magnolias honor Charles Baciagalupi and Howard Allen, wine-country veterans who provided the founders with early mentorship and guidance.

Set directly behind the hospitality building, the wine production facility is dug into the hillside below an expansive main terrace, an approach that not only provides passive cooling but minimizes the winery's visual impact on the site. The winery space is unassuming and straightforward yet flexible and supremely well equipped. While most wineries rent bottling and labeling equipment when it comes time to bottle, the team at Williams Selyem has its own bottling system, giving them the flexibility to bottle each wine just exactly when they deem it ready. Pressurized tanks similar to those you might see in a brewery push the wine along using inert gases and gravity rather than pulling it as is most commonly done. Jeff Mangahase and Patrick Bernard, winemaker and assistant winemaker, respective-ly, believe this method of moving the wine is gentler on the grapes.

Both owner and winemakers are dedicated to maintaining the wine-making style established by the original owners. The approach to winemaking is straight-forward, not fancy, and tradition is paramount—Jeff and Patrick strive to main-tain the wine-making traditions put in place by Burt and Ed. When Burt and Ed first started making wine, money was scarce, and they used what resources they could get their hands on. Since this is dairy country, old dairy pasteurizers were plentiful. Taking advantage of these castoffs, they cut them in half and used them to ferment the grapes. The current winemakers proudly point out that it's still done that way today.

OPPOSITE: Winery offices occupy the upper floor, shielded by the arching barrel-shaped roof.

ABOVE: A wall of frosted plexiglass floods the production room with light.

SAXUM
VINEYARDS

WINEMAKING IN THE CAVES

LOCATION: **PASO ROBLES**

ARCHITECTURE: **BK ARCHITECT / LAKE|FLATO / CLAYTON & LITTLE**

Justin Smith is Paso Robles's home-grown success story, rising from early beginnings making wine in his garage to become one of the most revered of a new generation of winemakers.

In 2010, Justin's 2007 James Berry Vineyard bottling was named *Wine Spectator's* Wine of the Year, effectively making it the number-one wine in the world. Justin has received a 100-point score from Robert Parker. He's had thirty-eight wines rated 95+. His wait list is years long. He's a risk taker not afraid to think outside the box. (He was one of the first to shut off his irrigation, dry-farming on hot, calcareous hillsides of Paso Robles.)

This "instant" success was anything but instant. Justin grew up in Paso Robles, a stone's throw from Saxum. Raised by a veterinarian turned grape-grower, he learned his techniques through years of trial and error. His focus is squarely on producing Rhone-style reds, all sourced from his vineyards, and from Bill and Liz Armstrong's Paderewski Vineyard.

Architect Brian Korte met Justin while working on the design for Bill and Liz's Epoch Winery, where Justin was consulting winemaker and, in Brian's words, "a rising superstar." At the time, Justin was making wine out of a concrete block addition to his house, just up the hill from where his winery now stands. Each admired the talent of the other and Justin told Brian, "When I build my own winery, I'll be calling you."

A few years later, Justin called. The two men met, sketched out their ideas during their first meeting, and pretty much held true to their initial instincts throughout the project. Justin was clear from the beginning that all winemaking would happen in the caves. If you are trying to make wines sustainably in this climate, caves simply make sense. Dug deep into the earth, they take advantage of passive cooling. They also provide plenty of room to cruise around on a skateboard—Justin's preferred mode of transportation.

Justin has the soil in his blood. *Saxum* is Latin for stone, and his Bone Rock Vineyard was named for the multitude of whale bones found there. So it is no surprise that he feels at home in the caves. His wine library is set deep within the hillside, at the very back of the caves' middle bore. The back wall is left bare to expose a multitude of fossils, and a pile of whale bones collected at the base of the wall is a reminder of the sea that once covered the land here—all evidence of the calcareous soils western Paso Robles shares with the Rhone region.

At just 2,000 square feet, the winery building is really a covering for the three-pronged cave. The open plan is about living, entertaining, and relaxing during breaks. Justin's lab is the kitchen, the meeting room doubles as a dining room, and the rest area takes the shape of a laid-back lounge covered in boho kilims and outfitted with a retro record player. Justin hosts guests (wine buyers and key members of his mailing list) in the lounge or around the dining room table. These spaces are really extensions of his home, perched just 154 steps up the hill.

"Justin really lives here," says Brian. "It's small, private, and an expression of his minimalist approach."

The structure is straightforward, defined by its simple and ruggedly beautiful palette of materials: steel left to weather, blackened steel polished to a high sheen, concrete, glass, and charred cypress. Unlike the finished steel in the interior, the exterior shoring walls are left unfinished to gain a burnt umber patina over time. A deep overhang protects the west-facing interior from the blazing afternoon sun. By the time the sun is low enough in the western sky to come screaming in under the "sombrero," it is screened and diffused by the vineyards.

Inside, the steel finishes are transformed into a sleek polished black. Vertical cypress battens are given a traditional Japanese charred-wood finish that renders the wood fire and rot resistant. The dark hues of the industrial materials are lifted by white oak built-ins constructed from a decommissioned foudre—an oversized wine cask that Justin had saved for just this purpose.

The bohemian vibe in the main lounge, with its kilim quilts, pillows, and a vinyl record collection, reflects Justin's personal aesthetic as well as his recognition that his hardworking team needs a place to chill out and rest. It's a refuge from the caves, where most of the winemaking work takes place. Though caves are beautiful, their acoustics can be deafening. The lounge, and its classic music collection, provide an escape from the din.

When the winery construction was nearly complete, Justin asked Brian to create a simple barn for equipment storage. He needed somewhere to "store his stuff" but also wanted a vehicle to power the winery. The result is a rustic structure, constructed of reclaimed oil field drilling pipes that were, in Brian's words, "already nice and rusty." The walls, constructed of perforated metal screens, let in natural light and give the structure a sense of transparency from the interior. The team assembled the barn doors from the misfit leftover panels from the winery's steel retaining walls, which had been left in the sun to age. On top of the barn, 192 solar modules generate 87 kilowatt hours of energy a year, enough to fully power the winery and vineyard wells.

Justin embodies the term *down-to-earth*. "He's a low-maintenance kind of guy," comments Brian, "and the design needed to go with that."

PREVIOUS OVERLEAF: The laid-back lounge, a place for the winemaker and his staff to kick back and relax, is covered in boho kilims and outfitted with a retro record player.

ABOVE: A broad arc of steel embedded into the hillside holds it back just enough to form a building pad, and the shoring walls extend and disappear into the hillside.

OPPOSITE: The view from the entry leads straight through to the cave, where the work takes place.

ABOVE: Justin Smith's lab is the kitchen, which he calls his "insane space."

Deep within the cave's central bore, library bottles are stacked inside the mouths of raw steel dredge pipes that Brian

The walls of the small ag barn, constructed of perforated metal screens, let in natural light and give the structure a sense of transparency.

HOURGLASS WINES

MODERNISM INSPIRED BY NATURE

LOCATION: **CALISTOGA** | ARCHITECTURE: **LUNDBERG DESIGN**

What if one of the most compelling wineries in California wasn't a winery at all but simply a cave and a roof tucked within the forested landscape in the upper Napa Valley? What if the client and architect were not only creators of wine and architecture but artists with a philosophical bent? What if the client was also a gifted musician, and the architect had been an English major in college before obtaining a graduate degree in architecture and, to top it all off, had a full-scale metal and woodworking shop incorporated into his architectural practice?

If all of this were true, you would be talking about Hourglass Wines, which is the brainchild of Carolyn and Jeff Smith and their architect, Olle Lundberg. The couple wanted their winery to be a celebration of contemporary Napa Valley, embodying their dedication to the valley, their vineyard, and their cutting-edge approach to winemaking. They also had a limited budget within which to make their statement. Jeff credits Carolyn with finding Olle's eponymous firm, drawn to his design philosophy of nature-inspired modernism.

The couple loves the story of their first meeting with their architect so much, they feature it on their website. At their first meeting, Carolyn handed Olle a photograph: a simple, Swedish barn—an example of the unadulterated agricultural style that clearly expressed its function. According to the story, Olle placed his thumb over the barn's small window, the building's only adornment, and said with a smile, "Now it's perfect." They had their architect.

According to Jeff Smith, "the hook was set" for him in the wine business at an early age. Raised in the wine country, Jeff recounts early family dinners with Jack Davies, founder of Schramsberg Estate, and working for the legendary Robert Mondavi in his early twenties (while simultaneously pursuing his passion for music). His father, Ned Smith, purchased the 6-acre Hourglass Vineyard in 1976, knowing he had found something special. An avid student of California wine with an encyclopedic knowledge of the history of winemaking in the Napa Valley, Jeff speaks eloquently about both the art and science of wine.

Adept with words, Jeff calls winemaking a "balancing act of art and science, modernism and traditionalism, wound with a good dose of passion, tempered by intellect." Both architecture and wine are a direct expression of terroir and function. "Wineries are such an interesting project type because there is no other project where the diagram of the building's relationship to the land is so direct," says Olle.

Together, they grappled with the problem of how to fulfill their goals within their budget. Then it came to Olle that they could turn the traditional winery model inside out, putting the mechanics of winemaking on full display. What about not building a winery at all, he suggested, but digging deep into the hillside to create a cave for tasting and cellaring, and devising a cantilevered roof to shield the winery workers and grapes from the elements? Jeff and Olle share an admiration for the beauty found in the mechanics of things. Creating a winery where the mechanics of both the wine-making process and the structure (what there is of it) are fully exposed enable them to celebrate those mechanics and elevate them to an artform.

Set amid the redwoods just off Napa's Silverado Trail, Hourglass Wines is an integral part of the landscape. (Olle jokingly calls this his best landscape architecture project.) Tucked into the base of the hillside, where the land curves upward like a cupped hand, the winery embraces the mountain and leaves the valley to the vineyards. The design team peeled back the base of the hillside to form a building pad and cave portals. Two concrete retaining walls slope gently down to nothing, simultaneously holding back the hill and forming the rear walls of the open-air winery. Overhead, a cantilevered roof composed of steel and plexiglass shields the crush pad from the elements. It looks, in profile, like a suspension bridge with its seventeen ribs aligned on axis with the vine rows.

At Hourglass, the cave takes on a particular significance: It is not only where the wines are cellared but where people gather to taste and experience the wines, deep within the mountain. Therefore, the portals needed to be celebrated. Olle asked Jeff and his team to save every bottle of wine they opened for a year. He would not tell them why but asked them to make sure their bottles were varied in size and color. Then Lundberg Design's fabrication team cut the bottles and installed them within the circular steel portal to create their own version of a stained-glass window. It became the winery's signature element.

In creating a minimalistic structure for making and tasting wine, the idea is that nature will, to some degree, take that structure back. The creeping fig that has begun to cover the retaining wall surrounding the cave's main portal is early evidence of that transition.

With a limited program, each detail takes on a greater significance. One example is the gunite that covers the walls of the cave. Noticing the arching corduroy pattern created by the boring machine, Jeff asked the operator to re-create that pattern throughout the cave, an amazing feat of artistry, particularly when you consider the size and clumsiness of the machine used to create the pattern. Deeper in the cave, where the tastings are held, the team left the walls unfinished, simply encased in a steel hog wire mesh. The result is a tasting experience that is about as close to the land as one can get.

Jeff describes "postmodern winemaking"—a term coined by Clark Smith in his book of the same name—as a stage beyond traditionalism and modernism where winemakers learn to balance new findings with old traditions and, in the process, discover and express the unique qualities of a place. For Hourglass Wines, that place is 6 acres in the upper Napa Valley. It is also a winery that consists of a cave, a roof, and the land.

PREVIOUS OVERLEAF: A portal handcrafted in Lundberg Design's studio from the ends of dozens of wine bottles is a celebration of wine and a contemporary version of a stained-glass window.

ABOVE: Within the minimalist vocabulary, each detail takes on a heightened degree of significance. Here the ribs of the roof are perfectly aligned with the vineyard rows.

ABOVE: Central to the design was the idea that, to some degree, nature would take the structure back, evidenced by the creeping fig that has begun to cover the retaining wall surrounding the cave's main portal.

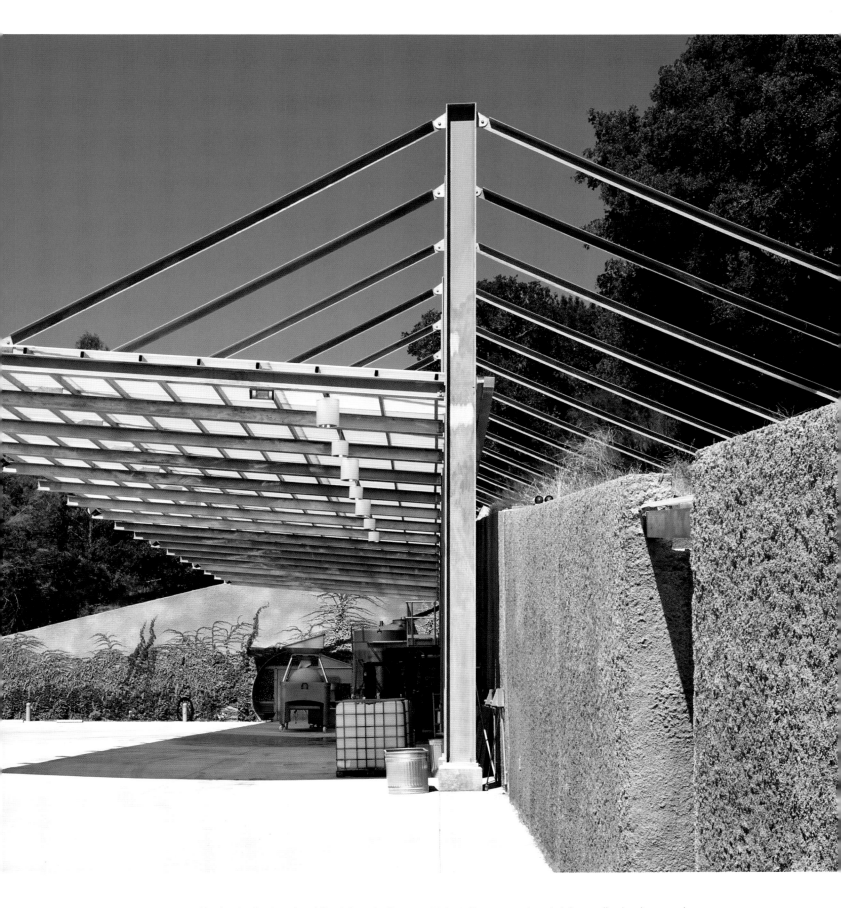

OPPOSITE: For both client and architect, beauty lies in the function of things, like the rhythm of the steel ribs that support the plexiglass roof.

ABOVE: Two concrete retaining walls simultaneously hold back the hillside and form the rear wall of the open-air winery. A cantilevered roof composed of steel ribs and plexiglass shields the crush pad from the elements.

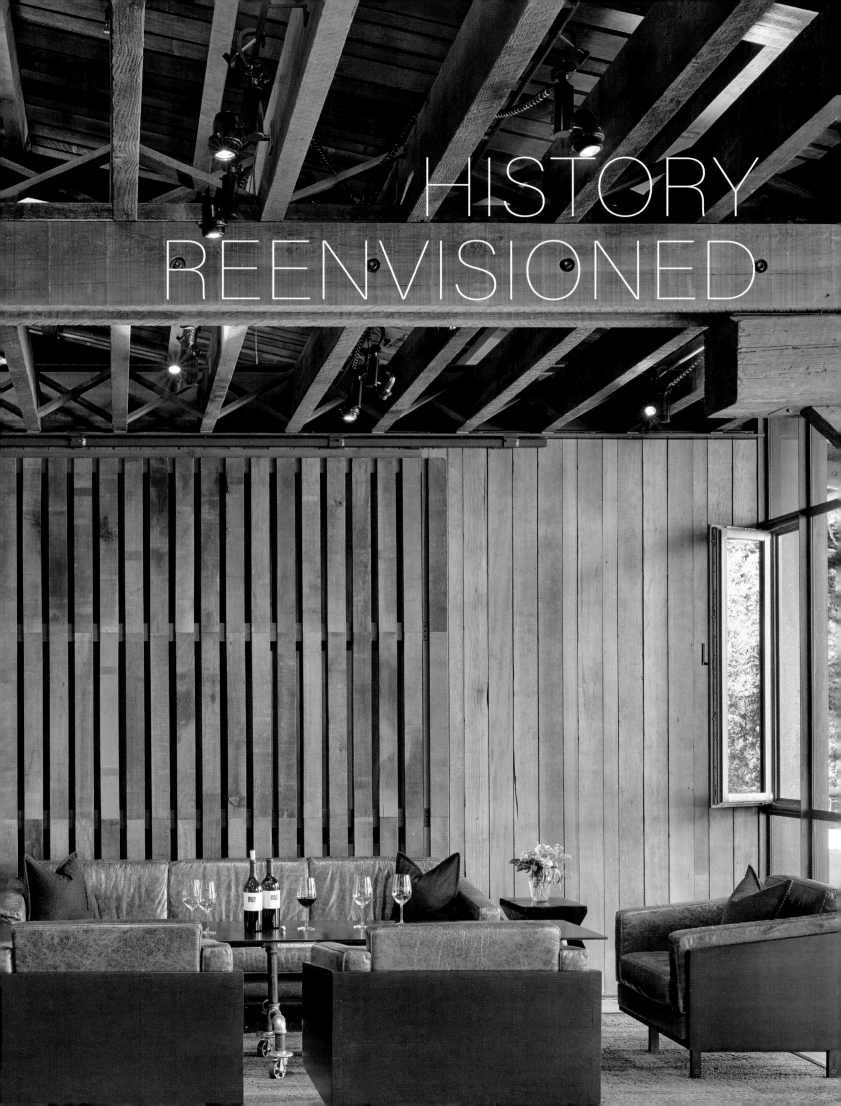

HISTORY
REENVISIONED

KISTLER VINEYARDS

A PURE EXPRESSION OF TERROIR

LOCATION: **FORESTVILLE** | ARCHITECTURE: **ARCHITECTURAL RESOURCES GROUP**

Set atop a knoll in the tiny wine country town of Forestville, Kistler Vineyards feels like something out of an agrarian fairytale. An all-white farmhouse with a sweeping stairway leads to several peaceful terraces, which step down the hill toward an idyllic pond and newly reconstructed barn.

Set behind a gate off a small road, Kistler Vineyards is private, like its founder and namesake, Steve Kistler. Dedicated to the craft of old-world winemaking, he planted all of his chardonnay vineyards from a single clone, developing every wine identically to allow the language of each plot to define the character of the wine. It is the purest possible expression of terroir. Steve planted his first vines on the property in 1978, with the first release of wine coming soon after in 1979. His Chardonnays and Pinot Noirs inspired a devoted following—some people have been on the list to purchase his wines since the 1980s.

When Bill Price purchased the winery in 2011, he knew he needed to introduce Kistler wines to a new generation of wine drinkers. The winery began to hold tastings by appointment only. Bill and Steve, along with Tom Bonomi (President and CFO of Price Family Wines) and Jason Kesner (assistant winemaker to Steve), began to lay plans

to create a visitor experience that captured the history and ethos of their approach to winemaking.

Working with Naomi Miroglio of Architectural Resources Group, they talked about what drove them: their dedication to the site and the purity of their wine-making. Every detail of the overall experience and journey through the two buildings, and the landscape between, was considered in minute detail. "They were so engaged, so committed. They have a great design sense, and they never lost focus," says Naomi.

They started with the farmhouse, renovating it in what they call "farmhouse with an edge." Though the layout has been altered, it still feels like walking into a traditional farmhouse living room with history in its bones. Before it was a home, it was a roadhouse, a raucous place with food served downstairs and a dance hall above.

At the back of the building, everything changes dramatically. An all-white tasting room spans the entire back of the building, opening up to embrace the surrounding views. "The all-white palette in the tasting room and upper level was Steve Kistler's idea, actually," says Naomi. "Once he put it on the table, we loved it and ran with it."

The 14-foot height of the distinctive entry doors is a classic proportion for barn doors, allowing forklifts carrying barrels to enter unimpeded.

Once the farmhouse was complete, they rolled right into the renovation of the barn. All of the materials had to be pure and unadulterated. Jason Kesner, who trained under Steve and took over as winemaker upon Steve's retirement from Kistler Vineyards at the end of 2017, took the lead on the design of the barn. He envisioned it as an expression of Kistler's unique wine-making process.

Upon entering the renovated barn, the very first impression is the aroma, which transports the visitor to the very heart of the wine-making experience. An almost physical presence, the aroma comes from the old barn wood, carefully saved from the original barn and repurposed to line the interior walls of the barn's soaring central space. The original intent was to use salvaged wood inside and out, but some of the barn's original siding was beyond saving. So the team changed their approach, reserving the salvaged wood (a combination of siding and timbers from the original barn and other salvaged timber) for the interior. New wood siding on the exterior is topped by the original metal roof. Outside comes inside, and old meets new.

When it came to the exterior, the team asked themselves, "What would a farmer do?" The answer was simple: he or she would go to Home Depot to buy siding. So that's what they did, and the result is beautifully simple and straightforward. The contrast between the new siding on the exterior and salvaged on the interior strikes just the right balance, and the mixture of salvaged sources creates a sense of randomness that makes it interesting.

Jason and Naomi advocated passionately for the 14-foot crimson doors that are arguably the barn's most distinctive feature. It took fortitude to hold onto this aspect of the design, but they had faith that the doors would become a defining feature. They were large, expensive, and heavy. The team met those challenges by using painted aluminum doors in place of the original steel, which allowed them to pick up the distinctive color from Kistler's Pinot Noir labels. The doors indeed have become the project's signature element.

"We were flexible when we needed to be, and inflexible when we knew it was important to stand firm, like holding out for those red doors," says Naomi.

The wine-tasting experience here includes a lesson in geology. Monitors take visitors through each of the vineyards, so they see the source of the wine they are tasting at the moment they taste it. A custom table runs the length of the barn's lofty central space, made of salvaged wood with a white strip of Corian embedded down the center, so visitors can more accurately see the color of the wine in their glasses when they hold them up. Windows set at just the right height provide views into the adjacent barrel rooms. No detail was overlooked.

In the barrel rooms on either side of the central space, gravel floors and stone walls encourage the growth of native yeasts and natural molds that make the Kistler wines distinctive. The process requires an intense amount of labor and a strong dose of faith, allowing nature to do what it will do. Many winemakers lose their courage partway through, but pushing through the entire process yields magical results, and in winemaking as well as architecture, dedication pays off.

PREVIOUS OVERLEAF: Salvaged from a number of sources, the varied widths and thicknesses of the reclaimed barn boards on the barn interior create a random pattern that is perfectly imperfect. The vertical orientation calls attention to the soaring interior volume.

ABOVE: Several inviting terraces step down the hill from the Trenton Roadhouse toward the idyllic pond and newly reconstructed barn.

OPPOSITE ABOVE: Set outside the tiny town of Forestville, Kistler Vineyards is imbued with the essence of a gentleman farmer—quietly grand yet humble.

OPPOSITE BELOW: Set adjacent to a small pond, the barn is covered in wood purchased from Home Depot, a decision sparked by the question "What would a farmer do?"

ABOVE: Kistler Vineyards feels like something out of an agrarian fairytale.

OPPOSITE: The upstairs tasting room was once a raucous dance hall. The all-white palette was Steve Kistler's idea, and the design team ran with it.

ABOVE: Entering the Trenton Roadhouse still feels like walking into a traditional farmhouse living room, with history in its bones.

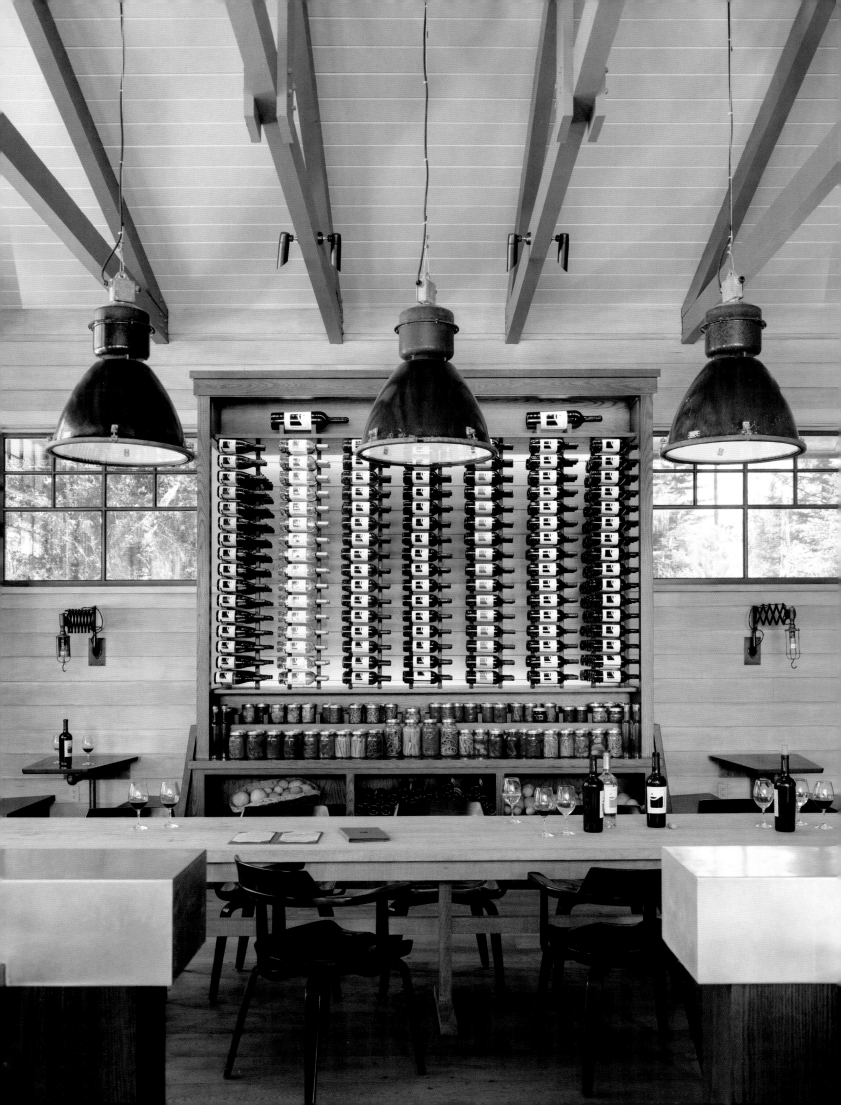

MEDLOCK AMES

SUSTAINABILITY AS A WAY OF LIFE

LOCATION: **ALEXANDER VALLEY** | ARCHITECTURE: **WADE DESIGN ARCHITECTS**

Set high in northeastern Sonoma County, Alexander Valley is famous for its unparalleled beauty. The 25-mile-long valley, 75 miles north of San Francisco, is off the beaten path for some, but to travel there is to be amply rewarded in both views and in wines.

Business partners Chris Medlock James and Ames Morrison began their wine journey far from the Alexander Valley. The two first became friends at Tulane University but went separate directions after college, Chris to New York for a job in finance and Ames for a multiyear stint in the Peace Corps. When Ames finished his work with the Peace Corps and joined Chris in New York (working as a teacher in the South Bronx), they remained best friends.

After a just few years in the city, Ames, who had grown up on a farm in Virginia, missed the land. The two, who had communed often over their love of wine, made the fateful decision to move west and make a go at winemaking. Chris provided the business know-how (he still works in finance in San Francisco) while Ames, with his background in agriculture, became the winemaker. What they shared was a deep dedication to sustainability as a way of life.

For two years, they looked at what seemed to them to be a hundred properties before finding their site in 1998, high atop Bell Mountain at the southern edge of the Alexander Valley. Here they created a sustainable Utopia–a 100 percent solar-powered, gravity-fed winery and biodynamically farmed vineyards. Going beyond organic farming, they embraced age-old low-impact farming methods, like animal husbandry, crop diversity, and what they proudly call "good, old-fashioned hard work." The co-owners chose to plant only 56 of the property's 338 acres with grapevines, devoting the rest to gardens and pastures or simply leaving the land the way they found it—covered in oaks, manzanitas, and wildflowers.

To say that the Bell Mountain vineyard is off the beaten track is an understatement, even in relatively remote Alexander Valley; so they began looking for a site to house a tasting room. Their search led them to the former Alexander Valley Store, set on a corner lot at the crossroads of the valley's two main roads. It had been a local watering hole for decades but was in disrepair and the victim of what Ames kindly calls "DIY building projects." Nevertheless, the building's importance to the history of the area had earned it a place on the historic register.

The site also had its challenges: the land was in need of rehabilitation, drainage was an issue, and space was at a premium on the scant one-acre parcel. Since the tasting room was disconnected from the winery, Chris and Ames wanted to make the experience about farming and the land, immersing visitors in their holistic environmental ethos by providing them a direct connection to working agriculture. They also wanted to acknowledge the building's history and connection to the local community.

To accomplish all this, the partners brought in a trio of designers to address the project in tandem, giving equal weight to the architecture, interiors, and landscape. Will Wick, of Wick Design, who had designed Chris's home, would orchestrate the interior design. Luke Wade, of Wade Design Architects, was brought on for his architectural aesthetic and, equally important, his technical prowess. Thomas Wolz, of Nelson Byrd Wolz, created a landscape that was a visual expression of the duo's agricultural and ecological ideals. True to those ideals, Chris and Ames hired Earthtone Construction to build the project; not accidentally, the company's mantra is "mindful building."

From the beginning, the team focused first on the landscape, fashioning an experience in which the interiors and landscape are integrally linked. This design transforms the flat site, which had once been used for ad hoc parking, into a series of outdoor rooms. The immersive experiences include an olive grove (created with trees saved and transplanted from groves that were giving over to other, more lucrative crops), an herb garden parterre composed of industrial steel raised planters, and a bocce-friendly courtyard of decomposed granite. At the center of it all lies a bioswale—which filters rainwater and redirects the site's problematic drainage—planted with wetland grasses. Set just beyond the tasting room terrace, the bioswale also provides a lovely wetland view. Each area brings visitors into direct contact with organic farming practices and regional native ecology.

The old store was dismantled and 80 percent of its parts were reused to create an open, airy space that is equal parts rustic-industrial and country schoolhouse with a mercantile vibe. The central tasting bar is open on all sides, surrounded by an array of seating options. The team agreed it was important to craft a space with a variety of interactions so guests can curate their own experience and level of engagement. The central bar, a communal table, smaller tables overlooking the terrace, and two kissing booths (for obvious reasons the most popular spot for couples) accommodate everything from couples to large groups comfortably in a relatively modest 2,000 square feet of space.

"This is really tasting in the round," says Luke. "There is barely any back-of-house, every face is public."

Overlooking the terrace, a wall of black steel triple-hung windows can be opened up in a number of ways to let the breeze flow through or raised entirely to create three open doorways. Although huge pocket doors might have been the more obvious call, the team wanted to maintain the vintage schoolhouse feel. "It's out in the country and it was a general store forever," says Luke, "it was important to maintain the history of the place." The historic mercantile atmosphere

PREVIOUS OVERLEAF: Medlock Ames highlights its wines and homemade wares in open shelving—a subtle reference to its history as a beloved country store.

ABOVE: The team worked closely together to make sure the building and landscape were inextricably linked.

ABOVE: A wall of triple-hung windows can be opened up in a number of ways to let the breeze flow through or raised entirely to create three open doorways.

OPPOSITE: A cross between a mercantile and a vintage schoolhouse, the interior has a variety of seating options to allow visitors to mix it up.

OPPOSITE ABOVE: The building's front facade reflects its history as the former Alexander Valley Store.

OPPOSITE BELOW: Nearly as large as the tasting room, the terrace is the lynchpin of the design, linking the wine-tasting experience with the organic gardens.

ABOVE: The tasting terrace and gardens bring visitors into direct contact with organic farming practices and regional native ecology.

LEFT: Built-in booths and found objects in the speakeasy reference a bygone era.

OPPOSITE: Hidden away through a private door, the former bar has been reimagined as a speakeasy, perfect for private groups and special events.

is further supported by the open shelving, vintage built-in refrigeration, lighting systems built from iron piping, and vintage factory light fixtures suspended over the communal table. A backlit bottle wall, lined below with house-made jams and olive oils, feels every bit like the country store it once was and to a degree still is.

The general store and bar were always run as separate businesses, and liquor laws require that they stay that way, which suits Chris and Ames just fine. Hidden away through a private door, the old bar was reimagined as a speakeasy which opens up when the tasting room shuts down. The dark wainscot and walls, built-in booths lined in velvet, a tin ceiling, and found objects are all newly installed, but they speak to a bygone era. Wanting a true connection to the history of the valley, Chris and Ames went to the historical society and, with their blessing, copied vintage photographs for the walls. Ames laughs when he recalls the night a bar patron took a look at one of the old photographs featuring bathing suit-clad women from the 1950s and declared, "That's my mom!"

The lynchpin of the project is the terrace. Nearly as large as the interior tasting room, it overlooks the landscape, shaded by a pergola covered in grapevines. These vines, however, are table grapes, destined to be made into the jams that line the shelves within. An extended eve is sistered on the steel channel to create a larger overhang, shading the walkway from the parking lot to the terrace. The resulting aesthetic is entirely appropriate, arising directly from a pragmatic solution. In Luke's capable hands, every challenge is an opportunity for a beautiful solution.

"What's cool is that this is where California is now," says Luke. "We're not importing an aesthetic, we're creating it."

EPOCH
ESTATE WINES

A LABOR OF LOVE ATOP A MAGICAL MOUNTAIN

LOCATION: **YORK MOUNTAIN, PASO ROBLES**

ARCHITECTURE: **LAKE|FLATO/BK ARCHITECT**

Set roughly halfway between Los Angeles and San Francisco, Paso Robles rests against the eastern foothills of the Santa Lucia Coastal Mountain Range. The town's full name, El Paso de Robles, means "passage of the oaks"—a tribute to the coast live oaks that populate the area's hills and valleys.

Set high in the coastal mountain range, in stark contrast to the gentle swales that make up much of Paso Robles wine country, the mountainous York Mountain American Viticultural Area (AVA) folds in on itself again and again as if the land had been crumpled up by some giant hand, then shaken back out again. Every slope here is different, resulting in a variety of microclimates that support a diverse array of flora: pines, coastal redwoods, grassy flower-filled meadows, and the iconic oaks that give Paso Robles its name.

Although York Mountain is one of California's smallest AVAs, it plays an outsized role in central California's wine-making history. Andrew York brought winemaking to the central coast in 1882 when he began planting vines and established the area's first winery on York Mountain. When Ignace Paderewski, a famous Polish statesman and concert pianist, purchased 2,000 acres in

Paso Robles's rolling hills, the central coast's reputation grew. Following Prohibition, Paderewski began to make his wine up in the hills at the York Mountain Winery.

As owners of both the former York Mountain Winery and Paderewski's original vineyards, Bill and Liz Armstrong are devoted stewards of the land and history in this corner of the world. Both geologists, they are extremely knowledgeable about every aspect of their property. Their search for the perfect site here in Paso Robles took seven or eight years, but when they finally found their site on York Mountain, they knew it was magical. Nonetheless, it took intense dedication and a clear vision to look at a crumbling ruin, felled by the San Simeon earthquake in 2003, and envision the jewel that it would become.

Set at the end of a winding country road lined on both sides by the sculptural forms of live oaks, the Epoch Estate Wines property is like a small village, with a collection of structures dissimilar but for their intent to preserve what was once there. The renovated farmhouse, a perfectly rustic horse barn (complete with the American flag painted on its roof), an original modular tasting room (now converted to an event space), two simply constructed

vineyard guest suites, and a contemporary wine production facility share the mountain site with the winery's most recent addition: a tasting room created from the ruins of the original York Mountain Winery.

Bill and Liz inspire deep devotion in their team, all of whom speak of the couple as if they are family. The two men at the helm of the new tasting room project, architect Brian Korte and Steve George, who served as the owner's representative and construction manager for the project, have been working with Bill and Liz for years. Steve started working with the family as an architect, then as a project manager, now as general manager and representative of just about everything Epoch. Brian has worked with the family for fourteen years (initially with Lake|Flato and later independently), working Bill's office—repurposed from a historic building in Denver—and on studies for numerous winery sites before finally completing the project on York Mountain.

The admiration of the Epoch team is mutual. "I think I am a frustrated architect, or maybe in a previous life I was an architect. So I have huge respect for functional beautiful buildings and the people that build them," says Bill. "I had the privilege of working with some really talented architects on this project. We all had similar visions regarding the love of the land and history. The meetings were always big fun. Lots of laughs and lots of wine help make a great building."

Restoring and rebuilding the original brick-and-stone structure was a painstaking process that took upwards of two years. The team took the original structure apart brick by brick and board by board. Every brick and stone from the original walls was meticulously tagged and numbered, then logged into a database so that the walls could be re-created exactly as they were. The team took pains to render the brickwork and coursing perfectly imperfect, reflecting how it would have originally been applied. Masonry workers used concrete to finish walls left ragged by the earthquake, letting the uneven edges tell the story of the structure that once stood there.

Every piece of wood used as cladding in the new structure was repurposed from the old, with the sole exception of the cladding on the ceiling (only because there simply was not enough original wood to go around). Brian hand-selected every piece, saving the best for areas—like the tasting bar counters, stair rails, and treads—where they could be polished and shown off. He also custom designed just about every aspect of the project, such as door handles fashioned from

PREVIOUS OVERLEAF: Bill and Liz Armstrong have given the historic winery back its voice and have returned winemaking to York Mountain.

ABOVE: The tasting room building seems to emerge from the meadow. Architect Brian Korte notes, "Buildings need to be subordinate to the land, not the other way around."

BELOW: Juxtaposition between the history of the stone and the new steel beams reinforcing the structure brings the beauty of the rough original materials into high relief.

OPPOSITE: Masonry workers used concrete to finish walls left ragged by the earthquake, letting the uneven edges tell the story of the structure that once stood here.

stacked leather washers, furnishings made of steel and reclaimed wood, and various doors and light fixtures. "This makes the project so personal for Bill and Liz because none of these things exist anywhere else," Brian says modestly.

The courtyard, part of the building's original footprint, emerged from under a collapsed roof. Rather than destroying this section of the building, the team elected to turn it into an outdoor tasting area surrounded by the vestiges of history: a massive original fireplace and stone walls, reinforced and left askew, the date 1893 scratched into one of the stones. Glass surrounding the stone calls attention to the crazy angle of the original wall. "The glass guys had fun with that one," laughs Steve.

To keep the wood-clad interiors from becoming too dark, broad expanses of glass on the front of the building draw light deep into the building. A clerestory window running above the tasting bar highlights the grassy hillside just behind it, and Ipe slats gracing the huge window at the end of the main tasting area dramatically frame the verdant hillside views beyond.

Both the historic tasting room building and the nearby wine production facility are a study in contrasts. The moody atmosphere of the tasting room's reclaimed wood interiors brings the surrounding green hills into sharp focus. The contemporary geometry and dark color of the structural steel reinforcements, set against a background of the rustic original materials, brings the beauty of both the new and the original elements into high relief. The production winery's clean lines and sharp edges stand in stark contrast to the sculptural majesty of the immense oaks visible from every window.

A clerestory window running above and behind the bar highlights the grassy hillside just behind it.

OPPOSITE ABOVE: The team documented and numbered every stone, logging the information into a database so that the walls could be re-created just as they were.

OPPOSITE BELOW: The nearly 1,500-pound winepress resides on joists above the tasting room, right where it would have done its work, long ago, on the original winery's upper floor.

ABOVE: Every architectural detail contributes to the immense richness of the palette: deep tones of reclaimed wood, golden stone, dark steel, and rough brick edged with concrete.

The cave, lit by two oculus skylights, dives
through the mountain at an angle to avoid the
roots of two large existing oaks.

Just up the hill from the new tasting room, the crisply contemporary form of the
new production facility has been carefully positioned amid a majestic oak grove.
"We placed the winery and barrel room in a manner that conformed with the land,"
asserts Bill. "Not one tree was damaged during the building of the winery, which
was quite a feat, as there are trees everywhere."

The barrel-vaulted cave, naturally lit by two dramatic oculus skylights, dives
straight through the mountain, emerging onto a meadow where a small school
once stood. (The Epoch team still refers to the meadow as "the schoolyard.")
Rather than cutting through the hillside at an easier 90-degree angle, the design
team sharply angled the cave to avoid the roots of two large oaks, successfully
preserving them.

The production facility is characterized by its restraint, a moving contrast of
rigid structural forms and wild organic undulations of the surrounding trees. The
team took an unassuming existing structure and reclad and reworked it over a tight
twelve-month construction timeframe to create a simple expression of functional
beauty. Burnished concrete masonry walls are topped with lightweight polycarbonate clerestory windows which, at the flip of a switch, open dramatically—all in
tandem—to ventilate the unconditioned space. The 15-foot doors of repurposed
redwood open to an orderly arrangement of steel tanks, kept free of the usual
safety rails through an ingenious rigging system that allows winemakers to rappel
down the tanks to do their work, practicing their mountain-climbing skills along
the way.

As he approaches the production building, Steve observes, "Wineries are the
new cathedrals." This structure constructed with straightforward agricultural
materials—burnished concrete masonry walls, polycarbonate sheeting, metal
cladding, and glass—certainly feels that way. A glass wall opens the upper story
meeting space (the team calls it the skybox) to the barrel room below, and huge
expanses of glass line the winemaker's office, the wine lab, and even the employee
breakroom, letting in views of the oaks in every direction.

Bill's goal is to make the best wine in the world, and his passion for the
wine-making process is matched by his commitment to the vision for his new
winery. Says Jordan Fiorentini, Epoch's winemaker, "Seldom is the winemaking so
revered that the lab is set on the prime view, right out front, but that's exactly the
way it is here." Jordan enjoys the best views at the winery, and the Epoch team's
reverence for the process is clear.

"This was a dream project for all of us," says Steve. "When we had a new idea
during the process, Bill never wavered. His only question was 'Is it better?' If the
answer was yes, then it was a go."

A view from the grassy slope highlights the transparency of the
new winery building.

DANA ESTATES

A SPIRIT OF GENEROSITY AND REBIRTH

LOCATION: **ST. HELENA**　　ARCHITECTURE: **BACKEN & GILLAM ARCHITECTS**

In Hindu and Buddhist practice, dana is the practice of cultivating generosity, and the lotus—which flowers on long stalks rooted deep in the earth —symbolizes purity of body, speech, and mind. The lotus flower also denotes rebirth. On each bottle of Dana Estates wine, twelve lotus flowers, standing in for the twelve months of the year, tell a story of the earth's continuing generosity. After providing their harvest and going dormant, the vines are reborn each spring, an annual echo of the rebirth of one of California's most hauntingly beautiful "ghost wineries."

California's ghost wineries are remnants of the state's wine-making history dating back to the mid-nineteenth century. At the dawn of the twentieth century, an outbreak of phylloxera, the 1906 earthquake, and then the double hit of Prohibition and the Great Depression nearly obliterated the wine industry. Most wineries disappeared; many were closed for decades before being renovated and reopened. Some continued to exist only as relics—walls built of durable Napa fieldstone abandoned amid the vineyards. Livingston Vineyards, with winery ruins dating from 1883 at its center, was one of those remaining ghost wineries waiting to be reborn.

Hi Sang Lee first visited the United States in the early 1970s. On that momentous trip a friend introduced him to wine, igniting a passion that led him to introduce wine culture to his native South Korea by establishing Nara Cellars, a fine wine importing company. Once he tasted Napa Valley Cabernet he knew he wanted it in his portfolio, and the Napa Valley quickly became his favorite among all the world's wine regions. He spent years visiting and building relationships with vintners throughout the Napa Valley, and is largely credited with establishing Korea's fine wine culture, nonexistent before the 1990s. Then in 2005, he fulfilled his dream with a winery of his own by purchasing Livingston Vineyards from John and Diane Livingston, who trusted Mr. Lee and his wife to protect the history and health of their land.

The Lees became the third stewards of the land, originally planted by German viticulturist H. W. Helms in 1883. Set at the northern end of the Rutherford Bench, the land is characterized not only by its beauty but by the quality of its soils. Rutherford Bench is the most well known of the Napa Valley's alluvial fans—with layers of gravel, soil, and silt from millions of years of erosion that provide the perfect combination of depth and drainage for the valley's famous Cabernet Sauvignon.

The Lees were introduced to Howard Backen and his firm, Backen & Gillam Architects, by Tom Shelton, a mutual friend. Tom, the former president and CEO at Joseph Phelps Vineyards, had been one of Mr. Lee's earliest clients as he established his wine import/export business, and they had remained friends ever since. Thorough in his process, Mr. Lee interviewed eleven architects before making his selection. Howard Backen was the only one who suggested they keep the ancient walls rather than demolishing them to make way for new structures. Moreover, he advocated leaving the stone walls unadorned to form an entry courtyard, allowing the full weight of their history and significance to resonate. It was clear that architect and client were aligned in their respect for the history imbued in the crumbling walls.

"Mr. Lee has great respect for things that have age and spirit," says Howard. "I wanted to put the sense of reverence back into the stone walls."

All that remained of the original winery were the stone walls of its eastern room and the three walls that now form the entry courtyard. The old walls had no foundation or even much of a stone floor, requiring an intricate effort to seismically retrofit and stabilize them. A new concrete trellis at the entry provides lateral support for the exterior walls that frame the courtyard. The team carefully dug a trench beneath the existing stone walls to pour concrete footings in place and placed a collar beam on top where it would be invisible from below. Cast-iron plates with a star pattern, part of the seismic retrofit of the stone, were cast from a plate the team found on site.

John Taft, a principal at Backen & Gillam, was instrumental in bringing Howard and Mr. Lee's vision for the new winery to life. His efforts have resulted in a composition of elements with a wonderful sense of geometry. A long pedestrian walkway set on axis with the arched entry allows visitors to approach slowly, progressing through vine rows under the newly constructed trellis, through an arched opening, and across the courtyard formed by the historic stone walls before eventually reaching the entry door. Stone patterning on the courtyard floor is a subtle reference to the traditional stone patterns found on the streets of Korea. Carried out in stones reclaimed from the flooding of China's Three Gorges Dam, the historic materials deepen the courtyard's very specific sense of place.

On either side of the courtyard, two symmetrical wings offer two distinct wine-tasting experiences. On one side, the more public of the two tasting rooms

PREVIOUS OVERLEAF: The approach to Dana Estate is a layered progression in which the visitor passes through vineyards, under a newly constructed trellis, past the historic stone walls, and across a courtyard, arriving finally at the winery entrance.

ABOVE: Architects Backen & Gillam carefully preserved the stone walls of this historic ghost winery, incorporating them into the design of a simple, agrarian structure that echoes the design of the original winery and the history of the area.

Cast-iron plates with a star pattern, part of the seismic retrofit of the stone, were cast from a plate the team found on-site.

is filled with light, the solid walls of stone counterbalanced by a massive opening that often characterizes the firm's designs. The entire wall of window lifts upward, opening up the room to fully embrace the courtyard.

The space that flanks the opposite side of the courtyard is entirely encased in stone, the soaring interior akin to a chapel. An internal structure of timber columns erected within the stone walls provides an exoskeleton of sorts to support the roof so that, although the roof rests atop the historic stone walls, they do not bear any of its weight. Subtly but dramatically backlit, the structural skeleton further emphasizes the room's lofty interior. The original foundation is clearly visible, a reminder of the building's age and history.

Tucked behind these buildings, the new production winery echoes the simple agrarian forms of the original stone structures, carried out entirely in board and batten stained an earthy shade of brown. Separate fermentation rooms hold custom-designed wood and concrete tanks. Throughout the winery, classical music serenades the grapes twenty-four hours a day as they mature into wine.

The foyer linking the two tasting wings opens, in turn, to the library: a rotunda encased in stained board-formed concrete and topped with a copper ceiling that holds the winery's most prized bottlings. The materials are soft and rich, but also strong and permanent, providing both reverence and protection for the valuable collection. The circular room captures the external axis that began at the pedestrian walkway and bends it toward the existing cave. "The cave has its own geometry," says Howard, "and we wanted to honor that."

At Dana Estates, the Lees strive to make the best wine in the world and, just as construction was nearing completion in 2009, the winery received its first perfect score—100 points given to the 2007 Lotus Vineyard Cabernet Sauvignon by Robert Parker. Referencing his client's quiet sense of humor, Howard recounts something Mr. Lee has told him many times: "Our wine will only be good when it is as good as this building, and we are not quite there yet."

Howard Backen counts Mr. Lee and the late Tom Shelton as two of his favorite people. In fact, Howard has a lot of favorite people, many of them his clients and former clients. When asked if all of his clients become his close friends, he laughs. "I think 98 percent of them do," he says. "I'm sure there is 2 percent that don't. I can't think of any offhand, but I'm sure they're out there."

OPPOSITE: In a dramatic design move, the full wall of windows in the main tasting room lifts upward to open the space to the courtyard.

ABOVE: The circular library captures the project's primary axis, which began at the pedestrian walkway, and bends it toward the existing cave.

JOSEPH PHELPS VINEYARDS

A DANCE WITH THE PAST

LOCATION: **ST. HELENA** | ARCHITECTURE: **BCV ARCHITECTURE + INTERIORS**

When architect Hans Baldauf, founding principal at San Francisco's BCV Architecture + Interiors, talks about his work transforming landmark buildings, he speaks about renewal, succession, responsibility, and stories. He describes it this way: "In these projects we find ourselves dancing with a building's past—a past we spend time coming to know so that we can reenvision the building for its new life." This process is different than a renovation, he explains, in which systems, functions, or even aesthetics are simply updated. It is the act of breathing new life into a building in order to take it into the next chapter of its history.

"A winery is both a factory and a house. It is really a locus for meaning. The architecture is important because it's the setting in which we affirm our stories," says Hans. "We are saving those stories."

Joseph Phelps built his eponymous winery on a 600-acre cattle ranch in Spring Valley in 1973, and it has since become an iconic architectural presence in the Napa Valley. Joe had founded Hensel Phelps Construction, building it into one of the largest and most successful construction companies in the United States. As both owner and contractor of Joseph Phelps Vineyards, Joe guided the vision for the original structure designed by the

preeminent Bay Area architect John Marsh Davis.

Within a grove of redwoods Joe had planted on an oak-studded slope with a commanding view of Spring Valley, Napa Valley, and the Mayacamas Mountains, the voluminous barn-like structure is at once timeless and an expression of its era. Comprised of two separate structures, the winery is characterized most strikingly by the massive wood trellis, set on axis with the view, that bisects the two matched barns. The building is a study in wood, a reflection of Joe's deep interest in the properties of the material and Davis's celebration of what Hans calls "the poetics of wood." Sheathed entirely in redwood, with a structure of Douglas fir, it is simultaneously monumental and inextricably connected to its natural surroundings.

The construction of the original winery was a very personal project. Everything was custom crafted on the property. Joe even set up a facility to manufacture every window and door on-site and used wood salvaged from the trusses of an old highway bridge in Gualala, on the Northern California coast, for the archetypal trellises. In recent years, winemaking and barrel storage had been shifted downhill to a new production building, giving the family the opportunity to rethink how

263

they would use the original property moving forward. The notion of what it is to visit a winery had evolved, and hospitality had become central to the experience.

Like so many wineries, Joseph Phelps Vineyards is an intergenerational endeavor. Joe's son Bill Phelps is now the executive chairman, and Bill's son Will is also involved. All three generations worked together to reenvision their winery. They engaged BCV Architecture + Interiors, respected for their work on landmark buildings, in conjunction with consulting designer Don Brandenberger to reinvent the original winery as an entirely new visitor experience. The resulting hospitality center provides an experience immersed in history and place, an enhanced food program, and offices for staff on a newly constructed second story set within the original structure.

The central question for the design team was "How does the winery evolve yet stay true to itself?" The answer was to focus on continuing the themes inherent in the design and history of the winery, while opening up the spaces to new uses and embracing the views. The design team kept the exterior of the buildings largely intact, working almost entirely within the volumes of the existing two-story structures. A new entry pathway leads to the original entry trellis, allowing visitors to experience for the first time the full drama of Davis's masterful composition. The team continued the structure's celebration of wood on the interior, with beautifully rendered interior trusses that reference the exterior trellis.

Winemaking is a long-term business. Accordingly, the redesign utilizes 17,000 square feet of the combined structures' 35,000 square feet, preserving space for further expansion by future generations. Within the established footprint, the team created a series of flexible spaces that allow for a broad range of uses.

The Great Hall, defined by two massive redwood trusses, lies at the heart of the north building. Paneled in board-on-board, rough-sawn Douglas fir, with five large light fixtures marching down the center, it is the new hospitality center's main living room and functions as an organizing space for the ground-floor tasting areas. Flanking the Great Hall, the Founder's Room and Library provide quiet spaces for private tastings. The Founder's Room and its terrace to the east, true to the name, celebrate the winery's founder, Joe Phelps. To the west lies the Library, where temperature-controlled casework protects and displays over forty years' worth of library wines. Encased in glass-and-blackened-steel doors and anchored by a round table of white and red elm so large it was brought into the room in pieces and then assembled on-site, the semitransparent room allows views from the Great Hall through the giant oblong barrels that line the adjacent Oval Room to the view beyond.

Added just four years after the original winery was constructed, the Oval Room, named for the shape of its oak barrels, runs along the building's western facade. Lined on one side by massive barrels and on the other with westerly views of the valley, this room more than any other provides the connective tissue linking history, wine, and place. The team preserved its sense of history while subtly rearranging the barrels to provide through views from the building's interior and further opening it up to the western terrace and its expansive valley vistas. Enhancing

PREVIOUS OVERLEAF: Architect Hans Baldauf calls Joseph Phelps Vineyards "a celebration of the poetics of wood."

ABOVE: The Great Hall, defined by its two massive redwood trusses, is the new hospitality center's main living room and primary organizing principle.

The design team repositioned the existing exterior trellis and realigned the interior's historic oval barrels to open up views through the interior and enhance the indoor-outdoor experience.

OPPOSITE: The reception vestibule, lined in shelves painted a creamy white, provides an airy contrast to the wood interiors through-out the rest of the building.

RIGHT: A private tasting room echoes the light tones of the reception vestibule.

the indoor-outdoor experience to the west was perhaps the most important element of the project. By expanding the terrace and landscape and repositioning the existing trellis, the team created a breadth of experience on the view.

One of the hallmarks of the original winery was a long shelf lining the upper walls of the vast space, which Joe Phelps used to display the empty bottles of significant wines that he and his family enjoyed at celebrations through the years. During the renovation, the bottles were meticulously cataloged and stored. They have been returned to their place of honor, set upon new redwood shelves that run the length of the Oval Room, a visual timeline of the Phelps family's wine-country history.

Hans Baldauf grew up visiting the wine country as its iconic wineries were coming into being in the 1960s and '70s. "What is interesting to me is that Napa wineries are now starting to have a history. It gives us an opportunity to look at architecture a bit differently," Hans remarks. The passage of time becomes a defining element in the way stories are told. At fifty years of age, buildings can be considered for listing on the National Register for Historic Places. Significant struc-tures in the Napa Valley are beginning to hit that mark. Robert Mondavi Winery, instrumental in bringing Napa Valley to the world stage, passed that mark in 2016. Joseph Phelps will reach it in just a few years.

"One of the things I love about our winery clients is that, because they are tied to the land, they are patient," says Hans. "They live by the rhythms of the land, so they have the patience for art and for craft, which take time. They build for the long run, and they understand the process of developing something over time."

OPPOSITE ABOVE: Inspired by the building's original entry trellis, the design team continued the building's celebration of wood on the interior.

OPPOSITE BELOW: The Oval Room, named for the distinctive shape of its barrels, is flanked on one side by the barrels and on the other by a bank of windows and French doors opening onto the expanded western terrace.

ABOVE: The design team redesigned the approach to the winery, inviting visitors to walk under the historic original trellis, through a sheltered courtyard, and into the new hospitality space.

LA CREMA ESTATE AT SARALEE'S VINEYARD

AN HOMAGE TO A BELOVED ICON

LOCATION: **RUSSIAN RIVER VALLEY** | ARCHITECTURE: **BRAYTONHUGHES DESIGN STUDIOS**

The daughter of a dairy farmer, Saralee Kunde was one of Sonoma County's most beloved citizens. She was an irresistible force for the celebration of Sonoma County agriculture and a generous philanthropist. Inducted into the Sonoma County Farm Bureau's Hall of Fame, she personified the Sonoma Valley with her warm and gracious spirit as well as her dedication to the region's agricultural heritage.

In 1988, Saralee and her husband, Richard, purchased a neglected 265-acre property along the Russian River. They wasted no time planting 68 acres of vines, including the eponymous Saralee's Vineyard. Richard hailed from deep grape-growing roots—his ancestors planted some of the region's first grapes in the 1880s and founded one of California's first bonded wineries. Together, the couple helped to establish the Russian River Valley as a premier cool-climate wine-growing region. They planted acres of gardens and opened their grounds to the community for fund-raisers of all kinds. Thousands of people raised millions of dollars for local causes thanks to the Kundes and their estate.

When it came time to sell, Saralee and Richard turned to Jackson Family Wines, another iconic wine-country family well known for its devotion to community, sustainability, and stewardship. Jackson Family Wines had sourced Pinot Noir and Chardonnay grapes from the Kundes for years and were a natural choice to shepherd the Kundes' legacy.

Nestled amidst acres of gardens and vineyards, the historic redwood barn that had once been Saralee's home was to become the centerpiece of the new La Crema Estate. Built in 1900 by a German immigrant who purchased the land for a whopping $9,000, the barn originally housed hops and horses, but the Kundes had transformed it into a residence overlooking the vineyards and surrounded by gardens. For its final transformation, Jackson Family Wines hired BraytonHughes Design Studios to create an elegant tasting experience within the carefully restored barn while maintaining a sense of intimacy that reminds visitors it was once home to two of Sonoma's most cherished citizens.

"Saralee Kunde's significance within the history and culture of Sonoma County was central to the ethos of the project," says Kiko Singh, principal at BraytonHughes Design Studios and the primary designer of La Crema Estate.

The restored barn is a fusion of residential and agrarian scale, a perfect marriage of rustic and

PREVIOUS OVERLEAF: The journey through the building takes visitors up the original circular stair. The intimate third-story spaces house private tasting areas.

ABOVE: New decks installed at every level ensure a fully integrated indoor-outdoor experience, no matter where guests find themselves.

refined. The soaring three-story structure is awe-inspiring in its height and intricacy, yet the furnishings are soft and inviting, with a modestly elegant finish that speaks to the La Crema identity.

"Our design brief was to infuse a feminine, sophisticated brand into a dark, rustic space," says Kiko. The design team achieved that balance through the use of light woods, soft textures, and pops of the signature La Crema red. Small window openings, particularly at the entry, make a light touch important. Not until visitors reach the rear of the building do they experience a flood of light and views through the expansive vineyard-facing windows.

Moving through the three-story barn feels like a journey, with distinct tasting experiences at every level. The entry, marked by a discrete sign and a set of rustic barn doors, is understated. The ground-level entry vestibule, with its low barn-board ceilings and muted light, feels like the living room it may have once been. Tucked at the rear of the building, a tasting room cloaked in cream walls and light wood provides a contemporary counterpoint to the historic entry, and the parade of windows provides visitors their first glimpse of the vineyard views.

The "wow" moment comes when guests ascend the barn's original circular stair, which at first obscures then gradually reveals the barn's towering volume. Custom light fixtures echo the building's vertical elements, and soft cove lighting calls attention to the beautiful rhythms of the exposed structural elements. Ringed with balconies, the grand space is reminiscent of a theater or a cathedral. Yet the second-story tasting space—a collected, residential-scale arrangement of furnishings designed for comfort—is warm and inviting. Soft surfaces, such as the leather-topped coffee tables, will develop patina and improve over time. Broad expanses of glass fill the space with light.

The sloping site allows a fourth level, set below the entry to open onto an expansive terrace. This space was once Richard Kunde's private domain, housing a full kitchen for him to indulge his love of cooking and entertaining. True to its original incarnation, it is now used to host food-centric events and private tastings.

The design team left the exterior of the barn largely as it was, with an important exception. Says Kiko, "We added decks at every level to ensure a fully integrated indoor-outdoor experience no matter where guests find themselves." Restrained in their proportions, the decks not only look as if they have always been there, but they make the facades of the original barn infinitely more interesting.

This classic barn, which has played such an integral role in the history and culture of Sonoma County, has been preserved much as it once was with its agricultural and residential roots firmly intact.

The design team left the exterior of the barn largely as it was, with the exception of new decks in both the front and back.

The three-story structure is awe-inspiring in its height and intricacy.
This is the building's "wow" moment.

OPPOSITE ABOVE: New decks on the rear facade offer beautiful views of the vineyards and gardens.

OPPOSITE BELOW: The residential scale and tone of the furnishings pay homage to the fact that this was once Saralee's home.

ABOVE: In the entry vestibule, a cozy sofa and wingback chairs flank a massive stone fireplace, original to the structure, and soft lighting provides subtle highlights.

ACKNOWLEDGMENTS

The New Architecture of Wine is a book I've been dreaming about for a long time. I'm forever grateful to those who were instrumental in helping me get it off the ground, and for many new friends I've made along the way.

My first thank-you must go to the owners and vintners, who so generously shared their stories with me, inviting me into their wineries and into their world. Their warmth and generosity of spirit made this journey a joy, and their passion for wine and the land is inspiring for us all. I've always loved the wine country; now I am truly hooked for life.

I'm grateful for the enthusiastic participation and support of the architects featured in this book: Alex Ceppi, Arcanum Architecture, Architectural Resources Group, Backen & Gillam Architects, BAR Architects, BCV, BK Architects, BraytonHughes Design Studios, Clayton & Little Architects, Gould Evans, Lake|Flato Architects, Lundberg Design, Matt Hollis Architects, Nielsen:Schuh Architects, Signum Architecture, Taylor Lombardo Architects, Wade Design Architects, and Walker Warner Architects. Their immense wealth of talent has been instrumental in defining the new architecture of wine in California. I am glad to know them all.

Sincere thanks to the photographers who so generously contributed their work to this book: Suzanne Becker Bronk, Bruce Damonte, Doug Dun (BAR Architects), Casey Dunn, Paul Dyer, Joe Fletcher, Adrian Gregorutti, Michael Hosfelt, Ryan Hughes (Lundberg Design), Matthew Millman, Erhard Pfeiffer, Cesar Rubio and David Wakely tell the story of these spectacular wineries with their images every bit as much as I tell it with my words. They bring to life on the page the owners' dreams, the architects' visions, and my stories. A special thanks to Matthew Millman for his beautiful front cover photograph, and to Casey Dunn for the stunning back cover image. I can't wait to work with them all again.

My father, Donald Sandy, FAIA, with whom I started my career in architecture, and with whom I am thrilled to share this new adventure in publishing, has been an inspiration. I am grateful for his beautiful sketches, which grace each of the chapters in the book. Not only is he an inspiration to me, but through his many decades of architectural practice he has been an inspiration to many of the architects featured in these pages.

I can't thank Gibbs Smith publisher enough for taking me on and publishing my first book. My editor, Madge Baird, provided her steady presence and sound counseling every step of the way. Designer Rita Sowins was not only talented but a joy to work with. Kenzie Quist, with her gift for copy editing, brought invaluable polish to the final product. I am indebted to my friend Chase Reynolds Ewald for introducing me to the team at Gibbs Smith.

My biggest debt of gratitude goes to my husband, Art, who never questioned that I could leave my in-house position after many decades to pursue my creative dreams. He believed in me even when I did not, at times, believe in myself. I owe the success of not only this book but my thriving brand consulting practice to him. Everyone deserves a spouse who is their biggest supporter, and I hit the jackpot.

Finally, I thank Lambert Bridge. Decades ago, in my early twenties, I visited this classic winery in the Dry Creek Valley with a group of friends. The modest redwood structure belies the soaring volume within. It was the first time I had tasted wine amid the wine barrels, and—lo and behold—there were chandeliers hung in the cavernous space, subtly transforming the interior into something different, a space in which wine and design worked together to create a bit of magic. There and then, all those years ago, I thought to myself, "Someday I'm going to write a book about wine and design."

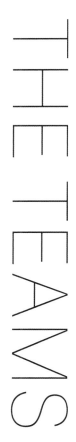

THE TEAMS

RAM'S GATE

LOCATION:
CARNEROS

ARCHITECTURE:
BACKEN & GILLAM ARCHITECTS / BGARCH.COM

INTERIOR DESIGN:
ORLANDO DIAZ-AZCUY / ODADA.NET

LANDSCAPE DESIGN:
CLAUDIA SCHMIDT LANDSCAPE DESIGN /
CLAUDIASCHMIDTLANDSCAPE.COM

CONSTRUCTION:
LEDCOR GROUP / LEDCOR.COM

PHOTOGRAPHY:
ADRIAN GREGORUTTI / GREGOPHOTO.COM

DAVIS ESTATES

LOCATION:
CARNEROS

ARCHITECTURE:
BACKEN & GILLAM ARCHITECTS / BGARCH.COM

INTERIOR DESIGN:
ORLANDO DIAZ-AZCUY / ODADA.NET

LANDSCAPE DESIGN:
CLAUDIA SCHMIDT LANDSCAPE DESIGN /
CLAUDIASCHMIDTLANDSCAPE.COM

CONSTRUCTION:
LEDCOR GROUP / LEDCOR.COM

PHOTOGRAPHY:
ADRIAN GREGORUTTI / GREGOPHOTO.COM

TRINCHERO NAPA VALLEY

LOCATION:
ST. HELENA

ARCHITECTURE:
BAR ARCHITECTS / BARARCH.COM

INTERIOR DESIGN:
ERIN MARTIN DESIGN / ERINMARTINDESIGN.COM

LANDSCAPE DESIGN:
SURFACE DESIGN / SURFACEDESIGN.COM

CONSTRUCTION:
FACILITY DEVELOPMENT COMPANY / FDC-COMP.COM

PHOTOGRAPHY:
MICHAEL

MacROSTIE WINERY

LOCATION:
HEALDSBURG

ARCHITECTURE:
GOULD EVANS / GOULDEVANS.COM

INTERIOR DESIGN:
GRANT K. GIBSON / GRANTKGIBSON.COM

LANDSCAPE DESIGN:
ROCHE + ROCHE / ROCHEANDROCHE.COM

CONSTRUCTION:
WRIGHT CONTRACTING / WRIGHTCONTRACTING.COM

PHOTOGRAPHY:
BRUCE DAMONTE / BRUCEDAMONTE.COM

MELKA ESTATES

LOCATION:
ST. HELENA

ARCHITECTURE:
SIGNUM ARCHITECTURE / SIGNUMARCHITECTURE.COM

INTERIOR DESIGN:
CHERIE MELKA / WITH SIGNUM ARCHITECTURE

LANDSCAPE DESIGN:
BLASEN LANDSCAPE ARCHITECTURE /
BLASENGARDENS.COM

CONSTRUCTION:
JASON HALL CONSTRUCTION INC

PHOTOGRAPHY:
ADRIAN GREGORUTTI / GREGOPHOTO.COM

QUINTESSA PAVILIONS

LOCATION:
ST. HELENA

ARCHITECTURE:
WALKER WARNER ARCHITECTS / WALKERWARNER.COM

INTERIOR DESIGN:
MACA HUNEEUS DESIGN / MACAHUNEEUS.COM

LANDSCAPE DESIGN:
LUTSKO ASSOCIATES / LUTSKOASSOCIATES.COM

CONSTRUCTION:
CELLO & MAUDRU CONTRACTORS /
CELLO-MAUDRU.COM

PHOTOGRAPHY:
MATTHEW MILLMAN / MATTHEWMILLMAN.COM

OCCIDENTAL WINES

LOCATION:
OCCIDENTAL

ARCHITECTURE:
NIELSEN:SCHUH / NIELSENSCHUH.COM

INTERIOR DESIGN:
NIELSEN:SCHUH ARCHITECTS / NIELSENSCHUH.COM

LANDSCAPE DESIGN:
NIELSEN:SCHUH / NIELSENSCHUH.COM

CONSTRUCTION:
GRACIE & ASSOCIATES, INC. /
GRASSIANDASSOCIATES.COM

PHOTOGRAPHY:
BRUCE DAMONTE / BRUCEDAMONTE.COM

PROGENY WINERY

LOCATION:
MT. VEEDER

ARCHITECTURE:
SIGNUM ARCHITECTURE /
SIGNUMARCHITECTURE.COM

INTERIOR DESIGN:
ANDREW FLESHER INTERIORS / ANDREWFLESHER.COM

LANDSCAPE DESIGN:
LUTSKO ASSOCIATES / LUTSKOASSOCIATES.COM

CONSTRUCTION:
GRASSI & ASSOCIATES INC. /
GRASSIANDASSOCIATES.COM

PHOTOGRAPHY:
ADRIAN GREGORUTTI / GREGOPHOTO.COM

PRESQU'ILE WINERY

LOCATION:
SANTA MARIA

ARCHITECTURE:
TAYLOR LOMBARDO / TAYLORLOMBARDO.COM

INTERIOR DESIGN:
KORPINEN ERICKSON INC.

LANDSCAPE DESIGN:
ARCADIA STUDIO / ARCADIA-LANDSCAPE.COM

CONSTRUCTION:
ROGERS & PEDERSEN CONSTRUCTION, INC. /
RP-CONSTRUCTION.COM

PHOTOGRAPHY:
ADRIAN GREGORUTTI / GREGOPHOTO.COM

CUVAISON ESTATE

LOCATION:
CARNEROS

ARCHITECTURE:
GOULD EVANS / GOULDEVANS.COM

INTERIOR DESIGN:
GOULD EVANS / GOULDEVANS.COM

LANDSCAPE DESIGN:
ROCHE + ROCHE / ROCHEANDROCHE.COM

CONSTRUCTION:
LEDCOR GROUP / LEDCOR.COM

PHOTOGRAPHY:
MATTHEW MILLMAN / MATTHEWMILLMAN.COM

HALL WINES

LOCATION:
ST. HELENA

ARCHITECTURE:
SIGNUM ARCHITECTURE / SIGNUMARCHITECTURE.COM

INTERIOR DESIGN:
NICOLE HOLLIS INTERIORS / NICOLEHOLLIS.COM

LANDSCAPE DESIGN:
OJB LANDSCAPE ARCHITECTURE / OJB.COM

CONSTRUCTION:
HATHAWAY DINWIDDIE / HDCCO.COM

PHOTOGRAPHY:
ADRIAN GREGORETTI / GREGOPHOTO.COM

CADE WINERY

LOCATION:
HOWELL MOUNTAIN

ARCHITECTURE:
SIGNUM ARCHITECTURE /
SIGNUMARCHITECTURE.COM

INTERIOR DESIGN:
SHOPWORKS

LANDSCAPE DESIGN:
SIGNUM ARCHITECTURE, ST. HELENA /
SIGNUMARCHITECTURE.COM

CONSTRUCTION:
GRASSI & ASSOCIATES INC. /
GRASSIANDASSOCIATES.COM

PHOTOGRAPHY:
ADRIAN GREGORUTTI / GREGOPHOTO.COM

THE TEAMS

LAW ESTATE WINES

LOCATION:
PASO ROBLES

ARCHITECTURE:
BAR ARCHITECTS / BARARCH.COM

INTERIOR DESIGN:
HBA SAN FRANCISCO / HBA.COM

LANDSCAPE DESIGN:
LUTSKO ASSOCIATES / LUTSKOASSOCIATES.COM,
MADRONE LANDSCAPES / MADRONELANDSCAPES.COM

CONSTRUCTION:
SPECIALTY CONSTRUCTION, INC. /
SPECIALTYCONSTRUCTION.COM

PHOTOGRAPHY:
DOUG DUN, BAR ARCHITECTS / BARARCH.COM

HAMEL FAMILY WINES

LOCATION:
SONOMA VALLEY

ARCHITECTURE:
GOULD EVANS / GOULDEVANS.COM

INTERIOR DESIGN:
ANGELA FREE DESIGN / ANGELAFREEDESIGN.COM

LANDSCAPE DESIGN:
JONATHAN PLANT & ASSOCIATES /
JONATHANPLANT.COM

CONSTRUCTION:
WRIGHT CONTRACTING / WRIGHTCONTRACTING.COM

PHOTOGRAPHY:
BRUCE DAMONTE / BRUCEDAMONTE.COM

STEWART CELLARS

LOCATION:
YOUNTVILLE

ARCHITECTURE:
ARCANUM ARCHITECTURE / ARCANUMARCHITECTURE.
COM

INTERIOR DESIGN:
KEN FULK / KENFULK.COM

LANDSCAPE DESIGN:
SURFACE DESIGN / SURFACEDESIGN.COM

CONSTRUCTION:
JIM MURPHY & ASSOCIATES / J-M-A.COM

PHOTOGRAPHY:
CESAR RUBIO / CESARRUBIO.COM

THE DONUM ESTATE

LOCATION:
CARNEROS

ARCHITECTURE:
MATT HOLLIS ARCHITECTS / MATTHOLLIS.COM

INTERIOR DESIGN:
MATT HOLLIS ARCHITECTS / MATTHOLLIS.COM

LANDSCAPE DESIGN:
CLEAVER DESIGN ASSOCIATES / CLEAVERDESIGN.COM

CONSTRUCTION:
KDC CONSTRUCTION / KDCCONSTRUCTION.COM

PHOTOGRAPHY:
CESAR RUBIO / CESARRUBIO.COM

WILLIAMS SELYEM WINERY

LOCATION:
HEALDSBURG

ARCHITECTURE:
ALEX CEPPI / D.ARC GROUP

INTERIOR DESIGN:
LAUREN BRANDWEIN DESIGN /
LAURENBRANDWEINDESIGN.COM

LANDSCAPE DESIGN:
WELBORN GROUP

CONSTRUCTION:
JIM MURPHY & ASSOCIATES / J-M-A.COM

PHOTOGRAPHY:
BRUCE DAMONTE / BRUCEDAMONTE.COM

SAXUM VINEYARDS

LOCATION:
PASO ROBLES

ARCHITECTURE:
LAKE|FLATO / LAKEFLATO.COM / CLAYTON & LITTLE /
CLAYTONANDLITTLE.COM / BK ARCHITECT

INTERIOR DESIGN:
LAKE/FLATO / LAKEFLATO.COM / CLAYTON & LITTLE /
CLAYTONANDLITTLE.COM / BK ARCHITECT

LANDSCAPE DESIGN:
MADRONE LANDSCAPES / MADRONELANDSCAPES.COM
(DESIGN/BUILD WITH SAXUM VINEYARDS)

CONSTRUCTION:
THE CONSTRUCTION ZONE /
THE-CONSTRUCTION-ZONE.COM

PHOTOGRAPHY:
CASEY DUNN / CASEYDUNN.NET

HOURGLASS WINES

LOCATION:
CALISTOGA

ARCHITECTURE:
LUNDBERG DESIGN / LUNDBERGDESIGN.COM

INTERIOR DESIGN:
LUNDBERG DESIGN / LUNDBERGDESIGN.COM

CONSTRUCTION:
CENTRIC GENERAL CONTRACTORS / CENTRICGC.COM

PHOTOGRAPHY:
RYAN HUGHES/LUNDBERG DESIGN

KISTLER VINEYARDS

LOCATION:
FORESTVILLE

ARCHITECTURE:
ARCHITECTURAL RESOURCES GROUP / ARGSF.COM

INTERIOR DESIGN:
ARCHITECTURAL RESOURCES GROUP / ARGSF.COM

LANDSCAPE DESIGN:
SURFACEDESIGN / SDISF.COM

CONSTRUCTION:
JIM MURPHY & ASSOCIATES / J-M-A.COM

PHOTOGRAPHY:
DAVID WAKELY / DAVIDWAKELY.COM

MEDLOCK AMES

LOCATION:
ALEXANDER VALLEY

ARCHITECTURE:
WADE DESIGN ARCHITECTS / WADE-DESIGN.COM

INTERIOR DESIGN:
WICK DESIGN GROUP / WICKDESIGN.COM

LANDSCAPE DESIGN:
NELSON BYRD WOLTZ / NBWLA.COM

CONSTRUCTION:
EARTHTONE CONSTRUCTION /
EARTHTONECONSTRUCTION.COM

PHOTOGRAPHY:
JOE FLETCHER / JOEFLETCHER.COM

EPOCH ESTATE WINES

LOCATION:
PASO ROBLES

ARCHITECTURE:
LAKE|FLATO / LAKEFLATO.COM / BK ARCHITECT

INTERIOR DESIGN:
LAKE|FLATO / LAKEFLATO.COM / BK ARCHITECT

LANDSCAPE DESIGN:
ANDREA COCHRAN LANDSCAPE ARCHITECTURE
(TASTING ROOM) / ACOCHRAN.COM

CONSTRUCTION:
THE CONSTRUCTION ZONE /
THE-CONSTRUCTION-ZONE.COM

PHOTOGRAPHY:
CASEY DUNN / CASEYDUNN.NET

DANA ESTATES

LOCATION:
ST. HELENA

ARCHITECTURE:
BACKEN & GILLAM ARCHITECTS / BGARCH.COM

INTERIOR DESIGN:
BACKEN & GILLAM ARCHITECTS / BGARCH.COM

LANDSCAPE DESIGN:
CLAUDIA SCHMIDT LANDSCAPE DESIGN /
CLAUDIASCHMIDTLANDSCAPE.COM

CONSTRUCTION:
LEDCOR GROUP / LEDCOR.COM

PHOTOGRAPHY:
ERHARD PFEIFFER / ERHARDPFEIFFER.COM

JOSEPH PHELPS VINEYARD

LOCATION:
ST. HELENA

ARCHITECTURE:
BCV ARCHITECTURE + INTERIORS / BCVARCH.COM

INTERIOR DESIGN:
BCV ARCHITECTURE + INTERIORS / BCVARCH.COM

LANDSCAPE DESIGN:
SMITH + SMITH / SMITH2.COM

CONSTRUCTION:
CELLO & MAUDRU CONSTRUCTION / CELLO-MAUDRU.COM

PHOTOGRAPHY:
BRUCE DAMONTE / BRUCEDAMONTE.COM

LA CREMA ESTATE
AT SARALEE'S VINEYARD

LOCATION:
RUSSIAN RIVER VALLEY

ARCHITECTURE:
BRAYTONHUGHES DESIGN STUDIOS / BHDSTUDIOS.COM

INTERIOR DESIGN:
BRAYTONHUGHES DESIGN STUDIOS / BHDSTUDIOS.COM

LANDSCAPE DESIGN:
LATE AFTERNOON GARDEN DESIGN /
LATEAFTERNOON.COM

CONSTRUCTION:
BRUCE TUCKER CONSTRUCTION /
BRUCETUCKERCONSTRUCTION.COM

PHOTOGRAPHY:
PAUL DYER / DYERPHOTO.COM

ABOUT THE AUTHOR

HEATHER SANDY HEBERT has spent her life immersed in literature, design, and wine. Raised in Marin County, at the southern edge of the wine country, she studied both literature and design and earned an MBA along the way. She spent over 25 years directing marketing for the San Francisco–based architecture firm founded by her father, Donald Sandy, FAIA. Throughout those years, she guided the firm's marketing and brand identity and wrote about the firm's multitude of projects, a great many of them in hospitality and wine. She left the firm in 2017 to pursue her love of storytelling and now works with numerous design, hospitality, and winery clients large and small to help them develop and convey their stories. *The New Architecture of Wine* is her first book. Heather lives in Marin County, California, with her husband and four children.